THIS CONTRACTOR LOG BOOK BELONGS TO:

Name:
....

Company:
....

Department:
....

Address:
....

....

....

Phone:
....

Fax:
....

Email:
....

Website:
....

CONTRACTOR LOG BOOK START & END DATE:

Log Book Number:
....

Log Book Start Date:
....

Log Book End Date:
....

Log Book Notes:
....

....

Log/Reference No	Badge No	Authorised By	Date

Contractors Name		Contractors Company Name	

Vehicle Reg No		Phone No / Mobile No		Email Address

Nature Of Work Undertaken		Location / Area Of Work	

Date	Contractor Time In	Contractor Time Out	Signature

Date	Keys/Key Fobs Time Out	Keys/Key Fobs Time In	Signature

Date Work Started	Time Work Started	Date Work Completed	Time Work Completed

Work Checked By		Date	Time

Important Notes	

Log/Reference No	Badge No	Authorised By	Date

Contractors Name		Contractors Company Name	

Vehicle Reg No		Phone No / Mobile No		Email Address

Nature Of Work Undertaken		Location / Area Of Work	

Date	Contractor Time In	Contractor Time Out	Signature

Date	Keys/Key Fobs Time Out	Keys/Key Fobs Time In	Signature

Date Work Started	Time Work Started	Date Work Completed	Time Work Completed

Work Checked By		Date	Time

Important Notes	

Log/Reference No		Badge No		Authorised By		Date	

Contractors Name			Contractors Company Name		

Vehicle Reg No		Phone No / Mobile No		Email Address	

Nature Of Work Undertaken			Location / Area Of Work		

Date	Contractor Time In	Contractor Time Out	Signature

Date	Keys/Key Fobs Time Out	Keys/Key Fobs Time In	Signature

Date Work Started	Time Work Started	Date Work Completed	Time Work Completed

Work Checked By		Date	Time

Important Notes	

Log/Reference No		Badge No		Authorised By		Date	

Contractors Name			Contractors Company Name		

Vehicle Reg No		Phone No / Mobile No		Email Address	

Nature Of Work Undertaken			Location / Area Of Work		

Date	Contractor Time In	Contractor Time Out	Signature

Date	Keys/Key Fobs Time Out	Keys/Key Fobs Time In	Signature

Date Work Started	Time Work Started	Date Work Completed	Time Work Completed

Work Checked By		Date	Time

Important Notes	

Log/Reference No		Badge No		Authorised By		Date	

Contractors Name		Contractors Company Name	

Vehicle Reg No		Phone No / Mobile No		Email Address	

Nature Of Work Undertaken		Location / Area Of Work	

Date	Contractor Time In	Contractor Time Out	Signature

Date	Keys/Key Fobs Time Out	Keys/Key Fobs Time In	Signature

Date Work Started	Time Work Started	Date Work Completed	Time Work Completed

Work Checked By		Date	Time

Important Notes	

Log/Reference No		Badge No		Authorised By		Date	

Contractors Name		Contractors Company Name	

Vehicle Reg No		Phone No / Mobile No		Email Address	

Nature Of Work Undertaken		Location / Area Of Work	

Date	Contractor Time In	Contractor Time Out	Signature

Date	Keys/Key Fobs Time Out	Keys/Key Fobs Time In	Signature

Date Work Started	Time Work Started	Date Work Completed	Time Work Completed

Work Checked By		Date	Time

Important Notes	

Log/Reference No	Badge No	Authorised By	Date

Contractors Name	Contractors Company Name

Vehicle Reg No	Phone No / Mobile No	Email Address

Nature Of Work Undertaken	Location / Area Of Work

Date	Contractor Time In	Contractor Time Out	Signature

Date	Keys/Key Fobs Time Out	Keys/Key Fobs Time In	Signature

Date Work Started	Time Work Started	Date Work Completed	Time Work Completed

Work Checked By	Date	Time

Important Notes	

Log/Reference No	Badge No	Authorised By	Date

Contractors Name	Contractors Company Name

Vehicle Reg No	Phone No / Mobile No	Email Address

Nature Of Work Undertaken	Location / Area Of Work

Date	Contractor Time In	Contractor Time Out	Signature

Date	Keys/Key Fobs Time Out	Keys/Key Fobs Time In	Signature

Date Work Started	Time Work Started	Date Work Completed	Time Work Completed

Work Checked By	Date	Time

Important Notes	

Log/Reference No	Badge No	Authorised By	Date

Contractors Name	Contractors Company Name

Vehicle Reg No	Phone No / Mobile No	Email Address

Nature Of Work Undertaken	Location / Area Of Work

Date	Contractor Time In	Contractor Time Out	Signature

Date	Keys/Key Fobs Time Out	Keys/Key Fobs Time In	Signature

Date Work Started	Time Work Started	Date Work Completed	Time Work Completed

Work Checked By	Date	Time

Important Notes	

Log/Reference No	Badge No	Authorised By	Date

Contractors Name	Contractors Company Name

Vehicle Reg No	Phone No / Mobile No	Email Address

Nature Of Work Undertaken	Location / Area Of Work

Date	Contractor Time In	Contractor Time Out	Signature

Date	Keys/Key Fobs Time Out	Keys/Key Fobs Time In	Signature

Date Work Started	Time Work Started	Date Work Completed	Time Work Completed

Work Checked By	Date	Time

Important Notes	

Log/Reference No	Badge No	Authorised By	Date

Contractors Name		Contractors Company Name	

Vehicle Reg No	Phone No / Mobile No		Email Address

Nature Of Work Undertaken		Location / Area Of Work	

Date	Contractor Time In	Contractor Time Out	Signature

Date	Keys/Key Fobs Time Out	Keys/Key Fobs Time In	Signature

Date Work Started	Time Work Started	Date Work Completed	Time Work Completed

Work Checked By		Date	Time

Important Notes	

Log/Reference No	Badge No	Authorised By	Date

Contractors Name		Contractors Company Name	

Vehicle Reg No	Phone No / Mobile No		Email Address

Nature Of Work Undertaken		Location / Area Of Work	

Date	Contractor Time In	Contractor Time Out	Signature

Date	Keys/Key Fobs Time Out	Keys/Key Fobs Time In	Signature

Date Work Started	Time Work Started	Date Work Completed	Time Work Completed

Work Checked By		Date	Time

Important Notes	

Log/Reference No		Badge No		Authorised By		Date	

Contractors Name	Contractors Company Name

Vehicle Reg No	Phone No / Mobile No	Email Address

Nature Of Work Undertaken	Location / Area Of Work

Date	Contractor Time In	Contractor Time Out	Signature

Date	Keys/Key Fobs Time Out	Keys/Key Fobs Time In	Signature

Date Work Started	Time Work Started	Date Work Completed	Time Work Completed

Work Checked By	Date	Time

Important Notes	

Log/Reference No		Badge No		Authorised By		Date	

Contractors Name	Contractors Company Name

Vehicle Reg No	Phone No / Mobile No	Email Address

Nature Of Work Undertaken	Location / Area Of Work

Date	Contractor Time In	Contractor Time Out	Signature

Date	Keys/Key Fobs Time Out	Keys/Key Fobs Time In	Signature

Date Work Started	Time Work Started	Date Work Completed	Time Work Completed

Work Checked By	Date	Time

Important Notes	

Log/Reference No	Badge No	Authorised By	Date

Contractors Name	Contractors Company Name

Vehicle Reg No	Phone No / Mobile No	Email Address

Nature Of Work Undertaken	Location / Area Of Work

Date	Contractor Time In	Contractor Time Out	Signature

Date	Keys/Key Fobs Time Out	Keys/Key Fobs Time In	Signature

Date Work Started	Time Work Started	Date Work Completed	Time Work Completed

Work Checked By	Date	Time

Important Notes	

Log/Reference No	Badge No	Authorised By	Date

Contractors Name	Contractors Company Name

Vehicle Reg No	Phone No / Mobile No	Email Address

Nature Of Work Undertaken	Location / Area Of Work

Date	Contractor Time In	Contractor Time Out	Signature

Date	Keys/Key Fobs Time Out	Keys/Key Fobs Time In	Signature

Date Work Started	Time Work Started	Date Work Completed	Time Work Completed

Work Checked By	Date	Time

Important Notes	

Log/Reference No	Badge No	Authorised By	Date

Contractors Name	Contractors Company Name

Vehicle Reg No	Phone No / Mobile No	Email Address

Nature Of Work Undertaken	Location / Area Of Work

Date	Contractor Time In	Contractor Time Out	Signature

Date	Keys/Key Fobs Time Out	Keys/Key Fobs Time In	Signature

Date Work Started	Time Work Started	Date Work Completed	Time Work Completed

Work Checked By	Date	Time

Important Notes	

Log/Reference No	Badge No	Authorised By	Date

Contractors Name	Contractors Company Name

Vehicle Reg No	Phone No / Mobile No	Email Address

Nature Of Work Undertaken	Location / Area Of Work

Date	Contractor Time In	Contractor Time Out	Signature

Date	Keys/Key Fobs Time Out	Keys/Key Fobs Time In	Signature

Date Work Started	Time Work Started	Date Work Completed	Time Work Completed

Work Checked By	Date	Time

Important Notes	

Log/Reference No	Badge No	Authorised By	Date

Contractors Name		Contractors Company Name	

Vehicle Reg No	Phone No / Mobile No	Email Address	

Nature Of Work Undertaken		Location / Area Of Work	

Date	Contractor Time In	Contractor Time Out	Signature

Date	Keys/Key Fobs Time Out	Keys/Key Fobs Time In	Signature

Date Work Started	Time Work Started	Date Work Completed	Time Work Completed

Work Checked By		Date	Time

Important Notes	

Log/Reference No	Badge No	Authorised By	Date

Contractors Name		Contractors Company Name	

Vehicle Reg No	Phone No / Mobile No	Email Address	

Nature Of Work Undertaken		Location / Area Of Work	

Date	Contractor Time In	Contractor Time Out	Signature

Date	Keys/Key Fobs Time Out	Keys/Key Fobs Time In	Signature

Date Work Started	Time Work Started	Date Work Completed	Time Work Completed

Work Checked By		Date	Time

Important Notes	

Log/Reference No	Badge No	Authorised By	Date

Contractors Name		Contractors Company Name	

Vehicle Reg No		Phone No / Mobile No	Email Address

Nature Of Work Undertaken		Location / Area Of Work	

Date	Contractor Time In	Contractor Time Out	Signature

Date	Keys/Key Fobs Time Out	Keys/Key Fobs Time In	Signature

Date Work Started	Time Work Started	Date Work Completed	Time Work Completed

Work Checked By		Date	Time

Important Notes	

Log/Reference No	Badge No	Authorised By	Date

Contractors Name		Contractors Company Name	

Vehicle Reg No		Phone No / Mobile No	Email Address

Nature Of Work Undertaken		Location / Area Of Work	

Date	Contractor Time In	Contractor Time Out	Signature

Date	Keys/Key Fobs Time Out	Keys/Key Fobs Time In	Signature

Date Work Started	Time Work Started	Date Work Completed	Time Work Completed

Work Checked By		Date	Time

Important Notes	

Log/Reference No	Badge No	Authorised By	Date

Contractors Name	Contractors Company Name

Vehicle Reg No	Phone No / Mobile No	Email Address

Nature Of Work Undertaken	Location / Area Of Work

Date	Contractor Time In	Contractor Time Out	Signature

Date	Keys/Key Fobs Time Out	Keys/Key Fobs Time In	Signature

Date Work Started	Time Work Started	Date Work Completed	Time Work Completed

Work Checked By	Date	Time

Important Notes	

Log/Reference No	Badge No	Authorised By	Date

Contractors Name	Contractors Company Name

Vehicle Reg No	Phone No / Mobile No	Email Address

Nature Of Work Undertaken	Location / Area Of Work

Date	Contractor Time In	Contractor Time Out	Signature

Date	Keys/Key Fobs Time Out	Keys/Key Fobs Time In	Signature

Date Work Started	Time Work Started	Date Work Completed	Time Work Completed

Work Checked By	Date	Time

Important Notes	

Log/Reference No	Badge No	Authorised By	Date

Contractors Name	Contractors Company Name

Vehicle Reg No	Phone No / Mobile No	Email Address

Nature Of Work Undertaken	Location / Area Of Work

Date	Contractor Time In	Contractor Time Out	Signature

Date	Keys/Key Fobs Time Out	Keys/Key Fobs Time In	Signature

Date Work Started	Time Work Started	Date Work Completed	Time Work Completed

Work Checked By	Date	Time

Important Notes	

Log/Reference No	Badge No	Authorised By	Date

Contractors Name	Contractors Company Name

Vehicle Reg No	Phone No / Mobile No	Email Address

Nature Of Work Undertaken	Location / Area Of Work

Date	Contractor Time In	Contractor Time Out	Signature

Date	Keys/Key Fobs Time Out	Keys/Key Fobs Time In	Signature

Date Work Started	Time Work Started	Date Work Completed	Time Work Completed

Work Checked By	Date	Time

Important Notes	

Log/Reference No	Badge No	Authorised By	Date

Contractors Name	Contractors Company Name

Vehicle Reg No	Phone No / Mobile No	Email Address

Nature Of Work Undertaken	Location / Area Of Work

Date	Contractor Time In	Contractor Time Out	Signature

Date	Keys/Key Fobs Time Out	Keys/Key Fobs Time In	Signature

Date Work Started	Time Work Started	Date Work Completed	Time Work Completed

Work Checked By	Date	Time

Important Notes	

Log/Reference No	Badge No	Authorised By	Date

Contractors Name	Contractors Company Name

Vehicle Reg No	Phone No / Mobile No	Email Address

Nature Of Work Undertaken	Location / Area Of Work

Date	Contractor Time In	Contractor Time Out	Signature

Date	Keys/Key Fobs Time Out	Keys/Key Fobs Time In	Signature

Date Work Started	Time Work Started	Date Work Completed	Time Work Completed

Work Checked By	Date	Time

Important Notes	

Log/Reference No	Badge No	Authorised By	Date

Contractors Name		Contractors Company Name	

Vehicle Reg No	Phone No / Mobile No	Email Address

Nature Of Work Undertaken		Location / Area Of Work	

Date	Contractor Time In	Contractor Time Out	Signature

Date	Keys/Key Fobs Time Out	Keys/Key Fobs Time In	Signature

Date Work Started	Time Work Started	Date Work Completed	Time Work Completed

Work Checked By		Date	Time

Important Notes	

Log/Reference No	Badge No	Authorised By	Date

Contractors Name		Contractors Company Name	

Vehicle Reg No	Phone No / Mobile No	Email Address

Nature Of Work Undertaken		Location / Area Of Work	

Date	Contractor Time In	Contractor Time Out	Signature

Date	Keys/Key Fobs Time Out	Keys/Key Fobs Time In	Signature

Date Work Started	Time Work Started	Date Work Completed	Time Work Completed

Work Checked By		Date	Time

Important Notes	

Log/Reference No	Badge No	Authorised By	Date

Contractors Name		Contractors Company Name	

Vehicle Reg No	Phone No / Mobile No	Email Address	

Nature Of Work Undertaken		Location / Area Of Work	

Date	Contractor Time In	Contractor Time Out	Signature

Date	Keys/Key Fobs Time Out	Keys/Key Fobs Time In	Signature

Date Work Started	Time Work Started	Date Work Completed	Time Work Completed

Work Checked By		Date	Time

Important Notes	

Log/Reference No	Badge No	Authorised By	Date

Contractors Name		Contractors Company Name	

Vehicle Reg No	Phone No / Mobile No	Email Address	

Nature Of Work Undertaken		Location / Area Of Work	

Date	Contractor Time In	Contractor Time Out	Signature

Date	Keys/Key Fobs Time Out	Keys/Key Fobs Time In	Signature

Date Work Started	Time Work Started	Date Work Completed	Time Work Completed

Work Checked By		Date	Time

Important Notes	

Log/Reference No	Badge No	Authorised By	Date

Contractors Name		Contractors Company Name	

Vehicle Reg No	Phone No / Mobile No	Email Address

Nature Of Work Undertaken		Location / Area Of Work	

Date	Contractor Time In	Contractor Time Out	Signature

Date	Keys/Key Fobs Time Out	Keys/Key Fobs Time In	Signature

Date Work Started	Time Work Started	Date Work Completed	Time Work Completed

Work Checked By		Date	Time

Important Notes	

Log/Reference No	Badge No	Authorised By	Date

Contractors Name		Contractors Company Name	

Vehicle Reg No	Phone No / Mobile No	Email Address

Nature Of Work Undertaken		Location / Area Of Work	

Date	Contractor Time In	Contractor Time Out	Signature

Date	Keys/Key Fobs Time Out	Keys/Key Fobs Time In	Signature

Date Work Started	Time Work Started	Date Work Completed	Time Work Completed

Work Checked By		Date	Time

Important Notes	

Log/Reference No	Badge No	Authorised By	Date

Contractors Name	Contractors Company Name

Vehicle Reg No	Phone No / Mobile No	Email Address

Nature Of Work Undertaken	Location / Area Of Work

Date	Contractor Time In	Contractor Time Out	Signature

Date	Keys/Key Fobs Time Out	Keys/Key Fobs Time In	Signature

Date Work Started	Time Work Started	Date Work Completed	Time Work Completed

Work Checked By	Date	Time

Important Notes	

Log/Reference No	Badge No	Authorised By	Date

Contractors Name	Contractors Company Name

Vehicle Reg No	Phone No / Mobile No	Email Address

Nature Of Work Undertaken	Location / Area Of Work

Date	Contractor Time In	Contractor Time Out	Signature

Date	Keys/Key Fobs Time Out	Keys/Key Fobs Time In	Signature

Date Work Started	Time Work Started	Date Work Completed	Time Work Completed

Work Checked By	Date	Time

Important Notes	

Log/Reference No	Badge No	Authorised By	Date

Contractors Name	Contractors Company Name

Vehicle Reg No	Phone No / Mobile No	Email Address

Nature Of Work Undertaken	Location / Area Of Work

Date	Contractor Time In	Contractor Time Out	Signature

Date	Keys/Key Fobs Time Out	Keys/Key Fobs Time In	Signature

Date Work Started	Time Work Started	Date Work Completed	Time Work Completed

Work Checked By	Date	Time

Important Notes	

Log/Reference No	Badge No	Authorised By	Date

Contractors Name	Contractors Company Name

Vehicle Reg No	Phone No / Mobile No	Email Address

Nature Of Work Undertaken	Location / Area Of Work

Date	Contractor Time In	Contractor Time Out	Signature

Date	Keys/Key Fobs Time Out	Keys/Key Fobs Time In	Signature

Date Work Started	Time Work Started	Date Work Completed	Time Work Completed

Work Checked By	Date	Time

Important Notes	

Log/Reference No	Badge No	Authorised By	Date

Contractors Name	Contractors Company Name

Vehicle Reg No	Phone No / Mobile No	Email Address

Nature Of Work Undertaken	Location / Area Of Work

Date	Contractor Time In	Contractor Time Out	Signature

Date	Keys/Key Fobs Time Out	Keys/Key Fobs Time In	Signature

Date Work Started	Time Work Started	Date Work Completed	Time Work Completed

Work Checked By	Date	Time

Important Notes	

Log/Reference No	Badge No	Authorised By	Date

Contractors Name	Contractors Company Name

Vehicle Reg No	Phone No / Mobile No	Email Address

Nature Of Work Undertaken	Location / Area Of Work

Date	Contractor Time In	Contractor Time Out	Signature

Date	Keys/Key Fobs Time Out	Keys/Key Fobs Time In	Signature

Date Work Started	Time Work Started	Date Work Completed	Time Work Completed

Work Checked By	Date	Time

Important Notes	

Log/Reference No	Badge No	Authorised By	Date

Contractors Name		Contractors Company Name	

Vehicle Reg No	Phone No / Mobile No	Email Address

Nature Of Work Undertaken		Location / Area Of Work	

Date	Contractor Time In	Contractor Time Out	Signature

Date	Keys/Key Fobs Time Out	Keys/Key Fobs Time In	Signature

Date Work Started	Time Work Started	Date Work Completed	Time Work Completed

Work Checked By		Date	Time

Important Notes	

Log/Reference No	Badge No	Authorised By	Date

Contractors Name		Contractors Company Name	

Vehicle Reg No	Phone No / Mobile No	Email Address

Nature Of Work Undertaken		Location / Area Of Work	

Date	Contractor Time In	Contractor Time Out	Signature

Date	Keys/Key Fobs Time Out	Keys/Key Fobs Time In	Signature

Date Work Started	Time Work Started	Date Work Completed	Time Work Completed

Work Checked By		Date	Time

Important Notes	

Log/Reference No	Badge No	Authorised By	Date

Contractors Name	Contractors Company Name

Vehicle Reg No	Phone No / Mobile No	Email Address

Nature Of Work Undertaken	Location / Area Of Work

Date	Contractor Time In	Contractor Time Out	Signature

Date	Keys/Key Fobs Time Out	Keys/Key Fobs Time In	Signature

Date Work Started	Time Work Started	Date Work Completed	Time Work Completed

Work Checked By	Date	Time

Important Notes	

Log/Reference No	Badge No	Authorised By	Date

Contractors Name	Contractors Company Name

Vehicle Reg No	Phone No / Mobile No	Email Address

Nature Of Work Undertaken	Location / Area Of Work

Date	Contractor Time In	Contractor Time Out	Signature

Date	Keys/Key Fobs Time Out	Keys/Key Fobs Time In	Signature

Date Work Started	Time Work Started	Date Work Completed	Time Work Completed

Work Checked By	Date	Time

Important Notes	

Log/Reference No	Badge No	Authorised By	Date

Contractors Name		Contractors Company Name	

Vehicle Reg No	Phone No / Mobile No	Email Address

Nature Of Work Undertaken		Location / Area Of Work	

Date	Contractor Time In	Contractor Time Out	Signature

Date	Keys/Key Fobs Time Out	Keys/Key Fobs Time In	Signature

Date Work Started	Time Work Started	Date Work Completed	Time Work Completed

Work Checked By		Date	Time

Important Notes	

Log/Reference No	Badge No	Authorised By	Date

Contractors Name		Contractors Company Name	

Vehicle Reg No	Phone No / Mobile No	Email Address

Nature Of Work Undertaken		Location / Area Of Work	

Date	Contractor Time In	Contractor Time Out	Signature

Date	Keys/Key Fobs Time Out	Keys/Key Fobs Time In	Signature

Date Work Started	Time Work Started	Date Work Completed	Time Work Completed

Work Checked By		Date	Time

Important Notes	

Log/Reference No	Badge No	Authorised By	Date

Contractors Name		Contractors Company Name	

Vehicle Reg No	Phone No / Mobile No	Email Address

Nature Of Work Undertaken		Location / Area Of Work	

Date	Contractor Time In	Contractor Time Out	Signature

Date	Keys/Key Fobs Time Out	Keys/Key Fobs Time In	Signature

Date Work Started	Time Work Started	Date Work Completed	Time Work Completed

Work Checked By		Date	Time

Important Notes	

Log/Reference No	Badge No	Authorised By	Date

Contractors Name		Contractors Company Name	

Vehicle Reg No	Phone No / Mobile No	Email Address

Nature Of Work Undertaken		Location / Area Of Work	

Date	Contractor Time In	Contractor Time Out	Signature

Date	Keys/Key Fobs Time Out	Keys/Key Fobs Time In	Signature

Date Work Started	Time Work Started	Date Work Completed	Time Work Completed

Work Checked By		Date	Time

Important Notes	

Log/Reference No	Badge No	Authorised By	Date

Contractors Name		Contractors Company Name	

Vehicle Reg No	Phone No / Mobile No	Email Address

Nature Of Work Undertaken		Location / Area Of Work	

Date	Contractor Time In	Contractor Time Out	Signature

Date	Keys/Key Fobs Time Out	Keys/Key Fobs Time In	Signature

Date Work Started	Time Work Started	Date Work Completed	Time Work Completed

Work Checked By		Date	Time

Important Notes	

Log/Reference No	Badge No	Authorised By	Date

Contractors Name		Contractors Company Name	

Vehicle Reg No	Phone No / Mobile No	Email Address

Nature Of Work Undertaken		Location / Area Of Work	

Date	Contractor Time In	Contractor Time Out	Signature

Date	Keys/Key Fobs Time Out	Keys/Key Fobs Time In	Signature

Date Work Started	Time Work Started	Date Work Completed	Time Work Completed

Work Checked By		Date	Time

Important Notes	

Log/Reference No	Badge No	Authorised By	Date

Contractors Name	Contractors Company Name

Vehicle Reg No	Phone No / Mobile No	Email Address

Nature Of Work Undertaken	Location / Area Of Work

Date	Contractor Time In	Contractor Time Out	Signature

Date	Keys/Key Fobs Time Out	Keys/Key Fobs Time In	Signature

Date Work Started	Time Work Started	Date Work Completed	Time Work Completed

Work Checked By	Date	Time

Important Notes	

Log/Reference No	Badge No	Authorised By	Date

Contractors Name	Contractors Company Name

Vehicle Reg No	Phone No / Mobile No	Email Address

Nature Of Work Undertaken	Location / Area Of Work

Date	Contractor Time In	Contractor Time Out	Signature

Date	Keys/Key Fobs Time Out	Keys/Key Fobs Time In	Signature

Date Work Started	Time Work Started	Date Work Completed	Time Work Completed

Work Checked By	Date	Time

Important Notes	

Log/Reference No	Badge No	Authorised By	Date

Contractors Name	Contractors Company Name

Vehicle Reg No	Phone No / Mobile No	Email Address

Nature Of Work Undertaken	Location / Area Of Work

Date	Contractor Time In	Contractor Time Out	Signature

Date	Keys/Key Fobs Time Out	Keys/Key Fobs Time In	Signature

Date Work Started	Time Work Started	Date Work Completed	Time Work Completed

Work Checked By	Date	Time

Important Notes	

Log/Reference No	Badge No	Authorised By	Date

Contractors Name	Contractors Company Name

Vehicle Reg No	Phone No / Mobile No	Email Address

Nature Of Work Undertaken	Location / Area Of Work

Date	Contractor Time In	Contractor Time Out	Signature

Date	Keys/Key Fobs Time Out	Keys/Key Fobs Time In	Signature

Date Work Started	Time Work Started	Date Work Completed	Time Work Completed

Work Checked By	Date	Time

Important Notes	

Log/Reference No	Badge No	Authorised By	Date

Contractors Name	Contractors Company Name

Vehicle Reg No	Phone No / Mobile No	Email Address

Nature Of Work Undertaken	Location / Area Of Work

Date	Contractor Time In	Contractor Time Out	Signature

Date	Keys/Key Fobs Time Out	Keys/Key Fobs Time In	Signature

Date Work Started	Time Work Started	Date Work Completed	Time Work Completed

Work Checked By	Date	Time

Important Notes	

Log/Reference No	Badge No	Authorised By	Date

Contractors Name	Contractors Company Name

Vehicle Reg No	Phone No / Mobile No	Email Address

Nature Of Work Undertaken	Location / Area Of Work

Date	Contractor Time In	Contractor Time Out	Signature

Date	Keys/Key Fobs Time Out	Keys/Key Fobs Time In	Signature

Date Work Started	Time Work Started	Date Work Completed	Time Work Completed

Work Checked By	Date	Time

Important Notes	

Log/Reference No	Badge No	Authorised By	Date

Contractors Name		Contractors Company Name	

Vehicle Reg No	Phone No / Mobile No	Email Address

Nature Of Work Undertaken	Location / Area Of Work

Date	Contractor Time In	Contractor Time Out	Signature

Date	Keys/Key Fobs Time Out	Keys/Key Fobs Time In	Signature

Date Work Started	Time Work Started	Date Work Completed	Time Work Completed

Work Checked By	Date	Time

Important Notes	

Log/Reference No	Badge No	Authorised By	Date

Contractors Name		Contractors Company Name	

Vehicle Reg No	Phone No / Mobile No	Email Address

Nature Of Work Undertaken	Location / Area Of Work

Date	Contractor Time In	Contractor Time Out	Signature

Date	Keys/Key Fobs Time Out	Keys/Key Fobs Time In	Signature

Date Work Started	Time Work Started	Date Work Completed	Time Work Completed

Work Checked By	Date	Time

Important Notes	

Log/Reference No		Badge No		Authorised By		Date	

Contractors Name				Contractors Company Name			

Vehicle Reg No		Phone No / Mobile No		Email Address	

Nature Of Work Undertaken				Location / Area Of Work			

Date	Contractor Time In	Contractor Time Out	Signature

Date	Keys/Key Fobs Time Out	Keys/Key Fobs Time In	Signature

Date Work Started	Time Work Started	Date Work Completed	Time Work Completed

Work Checked By		Date	Time

Important Notes	

Log/Reference No		Badge No		Authorised By		Date	

Contractors Name				Contractors Company Name			

Vehicle Reg No		Phone No / Mobile No		Email Address	

Nature Of Work Undertaken				Location / Area Of Work			

Date	Contractor Time In	Contractor Time Out	Signature

Date	Keys/Key Fobs Time Out	Keys/Key Fobs Time In	Signature

Date Work Started	Time Work Started	Date Work Completed	Time Work Completed

Work Checked By		Date	Time

Important Notes	

Log/Reference No	Badge No	Authorised By	Date

Contractors Name		Contractors Company Name	

Vehicle Reg No	Phone No / Mobile No	Email Address	

Nature Of Work Undertaken		Location / Area Of Work	

Date	Contractor Time In	Contractor Time Out	Signature

Date	Keys/Key Fobs Time Out	Keys/Key Fobs Time In	Signature

Date Work Started	Time Work Started	Date Work Completed	Time Work Completed

Work Checked By		Date	Time

Important Notes	

Log/Reference No	Badge No	Authorised By	Date

Contractors Name		Contractors Company Name	

Vehicle Reg No	Phone No / Mobile No	Email Address	

Nature Of Work Undertaken		Location / Area Of Work	

Date	Contractor Time In	Contractor Time Out	Signature

Date	Keys/Key Fobs Time Out	Keys/Key Fobs Time In	Signature

Date Work Started	Time Work Started	Date Work Completed	Time Work Completed

Work Checked By		Date	Time

Important Notes	

Log/Reference No	Badge No	Authorised By	Date

Contractors Name	Contractors Company Name

Vehicle Reg No	Phone No / Mobile No	Email Address

Nature Of Work Undertaken	Location / Area Of Work

Date	Contractor Time In	Contractor Time Out	Signature

Date	Keys/Key Fobs Time Out	Keys/Key Fobs Time In	Signature

Date Work Started	Time Work Started	Date Work Completed	Time Work Completed

Work Checked By	Date	Time

Important Notes	

Log/Reference No	Badge No	Authorised By	Date

Contractors Name	Contractors Company Name

Vehicle Reg No	Phone No / Mobile No	Email Address

Nature Of Work Undertaken	Location / Area Of Work

Date	Contractor Time In	Contractor Time Out	Signature

Date	Keys/Key Fobs Time Out	Keys/Key Fobs Time In	Signature

Date Work Started	Time Work Started	Date Work Completed	Time Work Completed

Work Checked By	Date	Time

Important Notes	

Log/Reference No	Badge No	Authorised By	Date

Contractors Name		Contractors Company Name	

Vehicle Reg No		Phone No / Mobile No	Email Address

Nature Of Work Undertaken		Location / Area Of Work	

Date	Contractor Time In	Contractor Time Out	Signature

Date	Keys/Key Fobs Time Out	Keys/Key Fobs Time In	Signature

Date Work Started	Time Work Started	Date Work Completed	Time Work Completed

Work Checked By		Date	Time

Important Notes	

Log/Reference No	Badge No	Authorised By	Date

Contractors Name		Contractors Company Name	

Vehicle Reg No		Phone No / Mobile No	Email Address

Nature Of Work Undertaken		Location / Area Of Work	

Date	Contractor Time In	Contractor Time Out	Signature

Date	Keys/Key Fobs Time Out	Keys/Key Fobs Time In	Signature

Date Work Started	Time Work Started	Date Work Completed	Time Work Completed

Work Checked By		Date	Time

Important Notes	

Log/Reference No	Badge No	Authorised By	Date

Contractors Name		Contractors Company Name	

Vehicle Reg No	Phone No / Mobile No	Email Address

Nature Of Work Undertaken		Location / Area Of Work	

Date	Contractor Time In	Contractor Time Out	Signature

Date	Keys/Key Fobs Time Out	Keys/Key Fobs Time In	Signature

Date Work Started	Time Work Started	Date Work Completed	Time Work Completed

Work Checked By		Date	Time

Important Notes	

Log/Reference No	Badge No	Authorised By	Date

Contractors Name		Contractors Company Name	

Vehicle Reg No	Phone No / Mobile No	Email Address

Nature Of Work Undertaken		Location / Area Of Work	

Date	Contractor Time In	Contractor Time Out	Signature

Date	Keys/Key Fobs Time Out	Keys/Key Fobs Time In	Signature

Date Work Started	Time Work Started	Date Work Completed	Time Work Completed

Work Checked By		Date	Time

Important Notes	

Log/Reference No	Badge No	Authorised By	Date

Contractors Name	Contractors Company Name

Vehicle Reg No	Phone No / Mobile No	Email Address

Nature Of Work Undertaken	Location / Area Of Work

Date	Contractor Time In	Contractor Time Out	Signature

Date	Keys/Key Fobs Time Out	Keys/Key Fobs Time In	Signature

Date Work Started	Time Work Started	Date Work Completed	Time Work Completed

Work Checked By	Date	Time

Important Notes	

Log/Reference No	Badge No	Authorised By	Date

Contractors Name	Contractors Company Name

Vehicle Reg No	Phone No / Mobile No	Email Address

Nature Of Work Undertaken	Location / Area Of Work

Date	Contractor Time In	Contractor Time Out	Signature

Date	Keys/Key Fobs Time Out	Keys/Key Fobs Time In	Signature

Date Work Started	Time Work Started	Date Work Completed	Time Work Completed

Work Checked By	Date	Time

Important Notes	

Log/Reference No	Badge No	Authorised By	Date

Contractors Name	Contractors Company Name

Vehicle Reg No	Phone No / Mobile No	Email Address

Nature Of Work Undertaken	Location / Area Of Work

Date	Contractor Time In	Contractor Time Out	Signature

Date	Keys/Key Fobs Time Out	Keys/Key Fobs Time In	Signature

Date Work Started	Time Work Started	Date Work Completed	Time Work Completed

Work Checked By	Date	Time

Important Notes	

Log/Reference No	Badge No	Authorised By	Date

Contractors Name	Contractors Company Name

Vehicle Reg No	Phone No / Mobile No	Email Address

Nature Of Work Undertaken	Location / Area Of Work

Date	Contractor Time In	Contractor Time Out	Signature

Date	Keys/Key Fobs Time Out	Keys/Key Fobs Time In	Signature

Date Work Started	Time Work Started	Date Work Completed	Time Work Completed

Work Checked By	Date	Time

Important Notes	

Log/Reference No	Badge No	Authorised By	Date

Contractors Name	Contractors Company Name

Vehicle Reg No	Phone No / Mobile No	Email Address

Nature Of Work Undertaken	Location / Area Of Work

Date	Contractor Time In	Contractor Time Out	Signature

Date	Keys/Key Fobs Time Out	Keys/Key Fobs Time In	Signature

Date Work Started	Time Work Started	Date Work Completed	Time Work Completed

Work Checked By	Date	Time

Important Notes	

Log/Reference No	Badge No	Authorised By	Date

Contractors Name	Contractors Company Name

Vehicle Reg No	Phone No / Mobile No	Email Address

Nature Of Work Undertaken	Location / Area Of Work

Date	Contractor Time In	Contractor Time Out	Signature

Date	Keys/Key Fobs Time Out	Keys/Key Fobs Time In	Signature

Date Work Started	Time Work Started	Date Work Completed	Time Work Completed

Work Checked By	Date	Time

Important Notes	

Log/Reference No	Badge No	Authorised By	Date

Contractors Name	Contractors Company Name

Vehicle Reg No	Phone No / Mobile No	Email Address

Nature Of Work Undertaken	Location / Area Of Work

Date	Contractor Time In	Contractor Time Out	Signature

Date	Keys/Key Fobs Time Out	Keys/Key Fobs Time In	Signature

Date Work Started	Time Work Started	Date Work Completed	Time Work Completed

Work Checked By	Date	Time

Important Notes	

Log/Reference No	Badge No	Authorised By	Date

Contractors Name	Contractors Company Name

Vehicle Reg No	Phone No / Mobile No	Email Address

Nature Of Work Undertaken	Location / Area Of Work

Date	Contractor Time In	Contractor Time Out	Signature

Date	Keys/Key Fobs Time Out	Keys/Key Fobs Time In	Signature

Date Work Started	Time Work Started	Date Work Completed	Time Work Completed

Work Checked By	Date	Time

Important Notes	

Log/Reference No	Badge No	Authorised By	Date

Contractors Name		Contractors Company Name	

Vehicle Reg No	Phone No / Mobile No	Email Address	

Nature Of Work Undertaken		Location / Area Of Work	

Date	Contractor Time In	Contractor Time Out	Signature

Date	Keys/Key Fobs Time Out	Keys/Key Fobs Time In	Signature

Date Work Started	Time Work Started	Date Work Completed	Time Work Completed

Work Checked By		Date	Time

Important Notes	

Log/Reference No	Badge No	Authorised By	Date

Contractors Name		Contractors Company Name	

Vehicle Reg No	Phone No / Mobile No	Email Address	

Nature Of Work Undertaken		Location / Area Of Work	

Date	Contractor Time In	Contractor Time Out	Signature

Date	Keys/Key Fobs Time Out	Keys/Key Fobs Time In	Signature

Date Work Started	Time Work Started	Date Work Completed	Time Work Completed

Work Checked By		Date	Time

Important Notes	

Log/Reference No	Badge No	Authorised By	Date

Contractors Name	Contractors Company Name

Vehicle Reg No	Phone No / Mobile No	Email Address

Nature Of Work Undertaken	Location / Area Of Work

Date	Contractor Time In	Contractor Time Out	Signature

Date	Keys/Key Fobs Time Out	Keys/Key Fobs Time In	Signature

Date Work Started	Time Work Started	Date Work Completed	Time Work Completed

Work Checked By	Date	Time

Important Notes	

Log/Reference No	Badge No	Authorised By	Date

Contractors Name	Contractors Company Name

Vehicle Reg No	Phone No / Mobile No	Email Address

Nature Of Work Undertaken	Location / Area Of Work

Date	Contractor Time In	Contractor Time Out	Signature

Date	Keys/Key Fobs Time Out	Keys/Key Fobs Time In	Signature

Date Work Started	Time Work Started	Date Work Completed	Time Work Completed

Work Checked By	Date	Time

Important Notes	

Log/Reference No	Badge No	Authorised By	Date

Contractors Name	Contractors Company Name

Vehicle Reg No	Phone No / Mobile No	Email Address

Nature Of Work Undertaken	Location / Area Of Work

Date	Contractor Time In	Contractor Time Out	Signature

Date	Keys/Key Fobs Time Out	Keys/Key Fobs Time In	Signature

Date Work Started	Time Work Started	Date Work Completed	Time Work Completed

Work Checked By	Date	Time

Important Notes	

Log/Reference No	Badge No	Authorised By	Date

Contractors Name	Contractors Company Name

Vehicle Reg No	Phone No / Mobile No	Email Address

Nature Of Work Undertaken	Location / Area Of Work

Date	Contractor Time In	Contractor Time Out	Signature

Date	Keys/Key Fobs Time Out	Keys/Key Fobs Time In	Signature

Date Work Started	Time Work Started	Date Work Completed	Time Work Completed

Work Checked By	Date	Time

Important Notes	

Log/Reference No	Badge No	Authorised By	Date

Contractors Name	Contractors Company Name

Vehicle Reg No	Phone No / Mobile No	Email Address

Nature Of Work Undertaken	Location / Area Of Work

Date	Contractor Time In	Contractor Time Out	Signature

Date	Keys/Key Fobs Time Out	Keys/Key Fobs Time In	Signature

Date Work Started	Time Work Started	Date Work Completed	Time Work Completed

Work Checked By	Date	Time

Important Notes	

Log/Reference No	Badge No	Authorised By	Date

Contractors Name	Contractors Company Name

Vehicle Reg No	Phone No / Mobile No	Email Address

Nature Of Work Undertaken	Location / Area Of Work

Date	Contractor Time In	Contractor Time Out	Signature

Date	Keys/Key Fobs Time Out	Keys/Key Fobs Time In	Signature

Date Work Started	Time Work Started	Date Work Completed	Time Work Completed

Work Checked By	Date	Time

Important Notes	

Log/Reference No	Badge No	Authorised By	Date

Contractors Name	Contractors Company Name

Vehicle Reg No	Phone No / Mobile No	Email Address

Nature Of Work Undertaken	Location / Area Of Work

Date	Contractor Time In	Contractor Time Out	Signature

Date	Keys/Key Fobs Time Out	Keys/Key Fobs Time In	Signature

Date Work Started	Time Work Started	Date Work Completed	Time Work Completed

Work Checked By	Date	Time

Important Notes	

Log/Reference No	Badge No	Authorised By	Date

Contractors Name	Contractors Company Name

Vehicle Reg No	Phone No / Mobile No	Email Address

Nature Of Work Undertaken	Location / Area Of Work

Date	Contractor Time In	Contractor Time Out	Signature

Date	Keys/Key Fobs Time Out	Keys/Key Fobs Time In	Signature

Date Work Started	Time Work Started	Date Work Completed	Time Work Completed

Work Checked By	Date	Time

Important Notes	

Log/Reference No	Badge No	Authorised By	Date

Contractors Name	Contractors Company Name

Vehicle Reg No	Phone No / Mobile No	Email Address

Nature Of Work Undertaken	Location / Area Of Work

Date	Contractor Time In	Contractor Time Out	Signature

Date	Keys/Key Fobs Time Out	Keys/Key Fobs Time In	Signature

Date Work Started	Time Work Started	Date Work Completed	Time Work Completed

Work Checked By	Date	Time

Important Notes	

Log/Reference No	Badge No	Authorised By	Date

Contractors Name	Contractors Company Name

Vehicle Reg No	Phone No / Mobile No	Email Address

Nature Of Work Undertaken	Location / Area Of Work

Date	Contractor Time In	Contractor Time Out	Signature

Date	Keys/Key Fobs Time Out	Keys/Key Fobs Time In	Signature

Date Work Started	Time Work Started	Date Work Completed	Time Work Completed

Work Checked By	Date	Time

Important Notes	

Log/Reference No	Badge No	Authorised By	Date

Contractors Name	Contractors Company Name

Vehicle Reg No	Phone No / Mobile No	Email Address

Nature Of Work Undertaken	Location / Area Of Work

Date	Contractor Time In	Contractor Time Out	Signature

Date	Keys/Key Fobs Time Out	Keys/Key Fobs Time In	Signature

Date Work Started	Time Work Started	Date Work Completed	Time Work Completed

Work Checked By	Date	Time

Important Notes	

Log/Reference No	Badge No	Authorised By	Date

Contractors Name	Contractors Company Name

Vehicle Reg No	Phone No / Mobile No	Email Address

Nature Of Work Undertaken	Location / Area Of Work

Date	Contractor Time In	Contractor Time Out	Signature

Date	Keys/Key Fobs Time Out	Keys/Key Fobs Time In	Signature

Date Work Started	Time Work Started	Date Work Completed	Time Work Completed

Work Checked By	Date	Time

Important Notes	

Log/Reference No	Badge No	Authorised By	Date

Contractors Name	Contractors Company Name

Vehicle Reg No	Phone No / Mobile No	Email Address

Nature Of Work Undertaken	Location / Area Of Work

Date	Contractor Time In	Contractor Time Out	Signature

Date	Keys/Key Fobs Time Out	Keys/Key Fobs Time In	Signature

Date Work Started	Time Work Started	Date Work Completed	Time Work Completed

Work Checked By	Date	Time

Important Notes	

Log/Reference No	Badge No	Authorised By	Date

Contractors Name	Contractors Company Name

Vehicle Reg No	Phone No / Mobile No	Email Address

Nature Of Work Undertaken	Location / Area Of Work

Date	Contractor Time In	Contractor Time Out	Signature

Date	Keys/Key Fobs Time Out	Keys/Key Fobs Time In	Signature

Date Work Started	Time Work Started	Date Work Completed	Time Work Completed

Work Checked By	Date	Time

Important Notes	

Log/Reference No	Badge No	Authorised By	Date

Contractors Name	Contractors Company Name

Vehicle Reg No	Phone No / Mobile No	Email Address

Nature Of Work Undertaken	Location / Area Of Work

Date	Contractor Time In	Contractor Time Out	Signature

Date	Keys/Key Fobs Time Out	Keys/Key Fobs Time In	Signature

Date Work Started	Time Work Started	Date Work Completed	Time Work Completed

Work Checked By	Date	Time

Important Notes	

Log/Reference No	Badge No	Authorised By	Date

Contractors Name	Contractors Company Name

Vehicle Reg No	Phone No / Mobile No	Email Address

Nature Of Work Undertaken	Location / Area Of Work

Date	Contractor Time In	Contractor Time Out	Signature

Date	Keys/Key Fobs Time Out	Keys/Key Fobs Time In	Signature

Date Work Started	Time Work Started	Date Work Completed	Time Work Completed

Work Checked By	Date	Time

Important Notes	

Log/Reference No	Badge No	Authorised By	Date

Contractors Name	Contractors Company Name

Vehicle Reg No	Phone No / Mobile No	Email Address

Nature Of Work Undertaken	Location / Area Of Work

Date	Contractor Time In	Contractor Time Out	Signature

Date	Keys/Key Fobs Time Out	Keys/Key Fobs Time In	Signature

Date Work Started	Time Work Started	Date Work Completed	Time Work Completed

Work Checked By	Date	Time

Important Notes	

Log/Reference No	Badge No	Authorised By	Date

Contractors Name	Contractors Company Name

Vehicle Reg No	Phone No / Mobile No	Email Address

Nature Of Work Undertaken	Location / Area Of Work

Date	Contractor Time In	Contractor Time Out	Signature

Date	Keys/Key Fobs Time Out	Keys/Key Fobs Time In	Signature

Date Work Started	Time Work Started	Date Work Completed	Time Work Completed

Work Checked By	Date	Time

Important Notes	

Log/Reference No	Badge No	Authorised By	Date

Contractors Name	Contractors Company Name

Vehicle Reg No	Phone No / Mobile No	Email Address

Nature Of Work Undertaken	Location / Area Of Work

Date	Contractor Time In	Contractor Time Out	Signature

Date	Keys/Key Fobs Time Out	Keys/Key Fobs Time In	Signature

Date Work Started	Time Work Started	Date Work Completed	Time Work Completed

Work Checked By	Date	Time

Important Notes	

Log/Reference No	Badge No	Authorised By	Date

Contractors Name	Contractors Company Name

Vehicle Reg No	Phone No / Mobile No	Email Address

Nature Of Work Undertaken	Location / Area Of Work

Date	Contractor Time In	Contractor Time Out	Signature

Date	Keys/Key Fobs Time Out	Keys/Key Fobs Time In	Signature

Date Work Started	Time Work Started	Date Work Completed	Time Work Completed

Work Checked By	Date	Time

Important Notes	

Log/Reference No	Badge No	Authorised By	Date

Contractors Name	Contractors Company Name

Vehicle Reg No	Phone No / Mobile No	Email Address

Nature Of Work Undertaken	Location / Area Of Work

Date	Contractor Time In	Contractor Time Out	Signature

Date	Keys/Key Fobs Time Out	Keys/Key Fobs Time In	Signature

Date Work Started	Time Work Started	Date Work Completed	Time Work Completed

Work Checked By	Date	Time

Important Notes	

Log/Reference No	Badge No	Authorised By	Date

Contractors Name	Contractors Company Name

Vehicle Reg No	Phone No / Mobile No	Email Address

Nature Of Work Undertaken	Location / Area Of Work

Date	Contractor Time In	Contractor Time Out	Signature

Date	Keys/Key Fobs Time Out	Keys/Key Fobs Time In	Signature

Date Work Started	Time Work Started	Date Work Completed	Time Work Completed

Work Checked By	Date	Time

Important Notes	

Log/Reference No	Badge No	Authorised By	Date

Contractors Name	Contractors Company Name

Vehicle Reg No	Phone No / Mobile No	Email Address

Nature Of Work Undertaken	Location / Area Of Work

Date	Contractor Time In	Contractor Time Out	Signature

Date	Keys/Key Fobs Time Out	Keys/Key Fobs Time In	Signature

Date Work Started	Time Work Started	Date Work Completed	Time Work Completed

Work Checked By	Date	Time

Important Notes	

Log/Reference No	Badge No	Authorised By	Date

Contractors Name	Contractors Company Name

Vehicle Reg No	Phone No / Mobile No	Email Address

Nature Of Work Undertaken	Location / Area Of Work

Date	Contractor Time In	Contractor Time Out	Signature

Date	Keys/Key Fobs Time Out	Keys/Key Fobs Time In	Signature

Date Work Started	Time Work Started	Date Work Completed	Time Work Completed

Work Checked By	Date	Time

Important Notes	

Log/Reference No	Badge No	Authorised By	Date

Contractors Name		Contractors Company Name	

Vehicle Reg No	Phone No / Mobile No	Email Address

Nature Of Work Undertaken		Location / Area Of Work	

Date	Contractor Time In	Contractor Time Out	Signature

Date	Keys/Key Fobs Time Out	Keys/Key Fobs Time In	Signature

Date Work Started	Time Work Started	Date Work Completed	Time Work Completed

Work Checked By		Date	Time

Important Notes	

Log/Reference No	Badge No	Authorised By	Date

Contractors Name		Contractors Company Name	

Vehicle Reg No	Phone No / Mobile No	Email Address

Nature Of Work Undertaken		Location / Area Of Work	

Date	Contractor Time In	Contractor Time Out	Signature

Date	Keys/Key Fobs Time Out	Keys/Key Fobs Time In	Signature

Date Work Started	Time Work Started	Date Work Completed	Time Work Completed

Work Checked By		Date	Time

Important Notes	

Log/Reference No	Badge No	Authorised By	Date

Contractors Name		Contractors Company Name	

Vehicle Reg No	Phone No / Mobile No	Email Address

Nature Of Work Undertaken		Location / Area Of Work	

Date	Contractor Time In	Contractor Time Out	Signature

Date	Keys/Key Fobs Time Out	Keys/Key Fobs Time In	Signature

Date Work Started	Time Work Started	Date Work Completed	Time Work Completed

Work Checked By		Date	Time

Important Notes	

Log/Reference No	Badge No	Authorised By	Date

Contractors Name		Contractors Company Name	

Vehicle Reg No	Phone No / Mobile No	Email Address

Nature Of Work Undertaken		Location / Area Of Work	

Date	Contractor Time In	Contractor Time Out	Signature

Date	Keys/Key Fobs Time Out	Keys/Key Fobs Time In	Signature

Date Work Started	Time Work Started	Date Work Completed	Time Work Completed

Work Checked By		Date	Time

Important Notes	

Log/Reference No	Badge No	Authorised By	Date

Contractors Name	Contractors Company Name

Vehicle Reg No	Phone No / Mobile No	Email Address

Nature Of Work Undertaken	Location / Area Of Work

Date	Contractor Time In	Contractor Time Out	Signature

Date	Keys/Key Fobs Time Out	Keys/Key Fobs Time In	Signature

Date Work Started	Time Work Started	Date Work Completed	Time Work Completed

Work Checked By	Date	Time

Important Notes	

Log/Reference No	Badge No	Authorised By	Date

Contractors Name	Contractors Company Name

Vehicle Reg No	Phone No / Mobile No	Email Address

Nature Of Work Undertaken	Location / Area Of Work

Date	Contractor Time In	Contractor Time Out	Signature

Date	Keys/Key Fobs Time Out	Keys/Key Fobs Time In	Signature

Date Work Started	Time Work Started	Date Work Completed	Time Work Completed

Work Checked By	Date	Time

Important Notes	

Log/Reference No	Badge No	Authorised By	Date

Contractors Name		Contractors Company Name	

Vehicle Reg No		Phone No / Mobile No	Email Address

Nature Of Work Undertaken		Location / Area Of Work	

Date	Contractor Time In	Contractor Time Out	Signature

Date	Keys/Key Fobs Time Out	Keys/Key Fobs Time In	Signature

Date Work Started	Time Work Started	Date Work Completed	Time Work Completed

Work Checked By		Date	Time

Important Notes	

Log/Reference No	Badge No	Authorised By	Date

Contractors Name		Contractors Company Name	

Vehicle Reg No		Phone No / Mobile No	Email Address

Nature Of Work Undertaken		Location / Area Of Work	

Date	Contractor Time In	Contractor Time Out	Signature

Date	Keys/Key Fobs Time Out	Keys/Key Fobs Time In	Signature

Date Work Started	Time Work Started	Date Work Completed	Time Work Completed

Work Checked By		Date	Time

Important Notes	

Log/Reference No	Badge No	Authorised By	Date

Contractors Name	Contractors Company Name

Vehicle Reg No	Phone No / Mobile No	Email Address

Nature Of Work Undertaken	Location / Area Of Work

Date	Contractor Time In	Contractor Time Out	Signature

Date	Keys/Key Fobs Time Out	Keys/Key Fobs Time In	Signature

Date Work Started	Time Work Started	Date Work Completed	Time Work Completed

Work Checked By	Date	Time

Important Notes	

Log/Reference No	Badge No	Authorised By	Date

Contractors Name	Contractors Company Name

Vehicle Reg No	Phone No / Mobile No	Email Address

Nature Of Work Undertaken	Location / Area Of Work

Date	Contractor Time In	Contractor Time Out	Signature

Date	Keys/Key Fobs Time Out	Keys/Key Fobs Time In	Signature

Date Work Started	Time Work Started	Date Work Completed	Time Work Completed

Work Checked By	Date	Time

Important Notes	

Log/Reference No	Badge No	Authorised By	Date

Contractors Name		Contractors Company Name	

Vehicle Reg No	Phone No / Mobile No	Email Address

Nature Of Work Undertaken		Location / Area Of Work	

Date	Contractor Time In	Contractor Time Out	Signature

Date	Keys/Key Fobs Time Out	Keys/Key Fobs Time In	Signature

Date Work Started	Time Work Started	Date Work Completed	Time Work Completed

Work Checked By		Date	Time

Important Notes	

Log/Reference No	Badge No	Authorised By	Date

Contractors Name		Contractors Company Name	

Vehicle Reg No	Phone No / Mobile No	Email Address

Nature Of Work Undertaken		Location / Area Of Work	

Date	Contractor Time In	Contractor Time Out	Signature

Date	Keys/Key Fobs Time Out	Keys/Key Fobs Time In	Signature

Date Work Started	Time Work Started	Date Work Completed	Time Work Completed

Work Checked By		Date	Time

Important Notes	

Log/Reference No	Badge No	Authorised By	Date

Contractors Name	Contractors Company Name

Vehicle Reg No	Phone No / Mobile No	Email Address

Nature Of Work Undertaken	Location / Area Of Work

Date	Contractor Time In	Contractor Time Out	Signature

Date	Keys/Key Fobs Time Out	Keys/Key Fobs Time In	Signature

Date Work Started	Time Work Started	Date Work Completed	Time Work Completed

Work Checked By	Date	Time

Important Notes	

Log/Reference No	Badge No	Authorised By	Date

Contractors Name	Contractors Company Name

Vehicle Reg No	Phone No / Mobile No	Email Address

Nature Of Work Undertaken	Location / Area Of Work

Date	Contractor Time In	Contractor Time Out	Signature

Date	Keys/Key Fobs Time Out	Keys/Key Fobs Time In	Signature

Date Work Started	Time Work Started	Date Work Completed	Time Work Completed

Work Checked By	Date	Time

Important Notes	

Log/Reference No	Badge No	Authorised By	Date

Contractors Name		Contractors Company Name	

Vehicle Reg No	Phone No / Mobile No	Email Address

Nature Of Work Undertaken		Location / Area Of Work	

Date	Contractor Time In	Contractor Time Out	Signature

Date	Keys/Key Fobs Time Out	Keys/Key Fobs Time In	Signature

Date Work Started	Time Work Started	Date Work Completed	Time Work Completed

Work Checked By		Date	Time

Important Notes	

Log/Reference No	Badge No	Authorised By	Date

Contractors Name		Contractors Company Name	

Vehicle Reg No	Phone No / Mobile No	Email Address

Nature Of Work Undertaken		Location / Area Of Work	

Date	Contractor Time In	Contractor Time Out	Signature

Date	Keys/Key Fobs Time Out	Keys/Key Fobs Time In	Signature

Date Work Started	Time Work Started	Date Work Completed	Time Work Completed

Work Checked By		Date	Time

Important Notes	

Log/Reference No	Badge No	Authorised By	Date

Contractors Name	Contractors Company Name

Vehicle Reg No	Phone No / Mobile No	Email Address

Nature Of Work Undertaken	Location / Area Of Work

Date	Contractor Time In	Contractor Time Out	Signature

Date	Keys/Key Fobs Time Out	Keys/Key Fobs Time In	Signature

Date Work Started	Time Work Started	Date Work Completed	Time Work Completed

Work Checked By	Date	Time

Important Notes	

Log/Reference No	Badge No	Authorised By	Date

Contractors Name	Contractors Company Name

Vehicle Reg No	Phone No / Mobile No	Email Address

Nature Of Work Undertaken	Location / Area Of Work

Date	Contractor Time In	Contractor Time Out	Signature

Date	Keys/Key Fobs Time Out	Keys/Key Fobs Time In	Signature

Date Work Started	Time Work Started	Date Work Completed	Time Work Completed

Work Checked By	Date	Time

Important Notes	

Log/Reference No	Badge No	Authorised By	Date

Contractors Name		Contractors Company Name	

Vehicle Reg No		Phone No / Mobile No	Email Address

Nature Of Work Undertaken		Location / Area Of Work	

Date	Contractor Time In	Contractor Time Out	Signature

Date	Keys/Key Fobs Time Out	Keys/Key Fobs Time In	Signature

Date Work Started	Time Work Started	Date Work Completed	Time Work Completed

Work Checked By		Date	Time

Important Notes	

Log/Reference No	Badge No	Authorised By	Date

Contractors Name		Contractors Company Name	

Vehicle Reg No		Phone No / Mobile No	Email Address

Nature Of Work Undertaken		Location / Area Of Work	

Date	Contractor Time In	Contractor Time Out	Signature

Date	Keys/Key Fobs Time Out	Keys/Key Fobs Time In	Signature

Date Work Started	Time Work Started	Date Work Completed	Time Work Completed

Work Checked By		Date	Time

Important Notes	

Log/Reference No	Badge No	Authorised By	Date

Contractors Name		Contractors Company Name	

Vehicle Reg No		Phone No / Mobile No		Email Address	

Nature Of Work Undertaken		Location / Area Of Work	

Date	Contractor Time In	Contractor Time Out	Signature

Date	Keys/Key Fobs Time Out	Keys/Key Fobs Time In	Signature

Date Work Started	Time Work Started	Date Work Completed	Time Work Completed

Work Checked By		Date	Time

Important Notes	

Log/Reference No	Badge No	Authorised By	Date

Contractors Name		Contractors Company Name	

Vehicle Reg No		Phone No / Mobile No		Email Address	

Nature Of Work Undertaken		Location / Area Of Work	

Date	Contractor Time In	Contractor Time Out	Signature

Date	Keys/Key Fobs Time Out	Keys/Key Fobs Time In	Signature

Date Work Started	Time Work Started	Date Work Completed	Time Work Completed

Work Checked By		Date	Time

Important Notes	

Log/Reference No	Badge No	Authorised By	Date

Contractors Name		Contractors Company Name	

Vehicle Reg No		Phone No / Mobile No	Email Address

Nature Of Work Undertaken		Location / Area Of Work	

Date	Contractor Time In	Contractor Time Out	Signature

Date	Keys/Key Fobs Time Out	Keys/Key Fobs Time In	Signature

Date Work Started	Time Work Started	Date Work Completed	Time Work Completed

Work Checked By		Date	Time

Important Notes	

Log/Reference No	Badge No	Authorised By	Date

Contractors Name		Contractors Company Name	

Vehicle Reg No		Phone No / Mobile No	Email Address

Nature Of Work Undertaken		Location / Area Of Work	

Date	Contractor Time In	Contractor Time Out	Signature

Date	Keys/Key Fobs Time Out	Keys/Key Fobs Time In	Signature

Date Work Started	Time Work Started	Date Work Completed	Time Work Completed

Work Checked By		Date	Time

Important Notes	

Log/Reference No	Badge No	Authorised By	Date

Contractors Name	Contractors Company Name

Vehicle Reg No	Phone No / Mobile No	Email Address

Nature Of Work Undertaken	Location / Area Of Work

Date	Contractor Time In	Contractor Time Out	Signature

Date	Keys/Key Fobs Time Out	Keys/Key Fobs Time In	Signature

Date Work Started	Time Work Started	Date Work Completed	Time Work Completed

Work Checked By	Date	Time

Important Notes	

Log/Reference No	Badge No	Authorised By	Date

Contractors Name	Contractors Company Name

Vehicle Reg No	Phone No / Mobile No	Email Address

Nature Of Work Undertaken	Location / Area Of Work

Date	Contractor Time In	Contractor Time Out	Signature

Date	Keys/Key Fobs Time Out	Keys/Key Fobs Time In	Signature

Date Work Started	Time Work Started	Date Work Completed	Time Work Completed

Work Checked By	Date	Time

Important Notes	

Log/Reference No	Badge No	Authorised By	Date

Contractors Name	Contractors Company Name

Vehicle Reg No	Phone No / Mobile No	Email Address

Nature Of Work Undertaken	Location / Area Of Work

Date	Contractor Time In	Contractor Time Out	Signature

Date	Keys/Key Fobs Time Out	Keys/Key Fobs Time In	Signature

Date Work Started	Time Work Started	Date Work Completed	Time Work Completed

Work Checked By	Date	Time

Important Notes	

Log/Reference No	Badge No	Authorised By	Date

Contractors Name	Contractors Company Name

Vehicle Reg No	Phone No / Mobile No	Email Address

Nature Of Work Undertaken	Location / Area Of Work

Date	Contractor Time In	Contractor Time Out	Signature

Date	Keys/Key Fobs Time Out	Keys/Key Fobs Time In	Signature

Date Work Started	Time Work Started	Date Work Completed	Time Work Completed

Work Checked By	Date	Time

Important Notes	

Log/Reference No	Badge No	Authorised By	Date

Contractors Name	Contractors Company Name

Vehicle Reg No	Phone No / Mobile No	Email Address

Nature Of Work Undertaken	Location / Area Of Work

Date	Contractor Time In	Contractor Time Out	Signature

Date	Keys/Key Fobs Time Out	Keys/Key Fobs Time In	Signature

Date Work Started	Time Work Started	Date Work Completed	Time Work Completed

Work Checked By	Date	Time

Important Notes	

Log/Reference No	Badge No	Authorised By	Date

Contractors Name	Contractors Company Name

Vehicle Reg No	Phone No / Mobile No	Email Address

Nature Of Work Undertaken	Location / Area Of Work

Date	Contractor Time In	Contractor Time Out	Signature

Date	Keys/Key Fobs Time Out	Keys/Key Fobs Time In	Signature

Date Work Started	Time Work Started	Date Work Completed	Time Work Completed

Work Checked By	Date	Time

Important Notes	

Log/Reference No	Badge No	Authorised By	Date

Contractors Name		Contractors Company Name	

Vehicle Reg No	Phone No / Mobile No	Email Address

Nature Of Work Undertaken	Location / Area Of Work

Date	Contractor Time In	Contractor Time Out	Signature

Date	Keys/Key Fobs Time Out	Keys/Key Fobs Time In	Signature

Date Work Started	Time Work Started	Date Work Completed	Time Work Completed

Work Checked By	Date	Time

Important Notes	

Log/Reference No	Badge No	Authorised By	Date

Contractors Name		Contractors Company Name	

Vehicle Reg No	Phone No / Mobile No	Email Address

Nature Of Work Undertaken	Location / Area Of Work

Date	Contractor Time In	Contractor Time Out	Signature

Date	Keys/Key Fobs Time Out	Keys/Key Fobs Time In	Signature

Date Work Started	Time Work Started	Date Work Completed	Time Work Completed

Work Checked By	Date	Time

Important Notes	

Log/Reference No	Badge No	Authorised By	Date

Contractors Name	Contractors Company Name

Vehicle Reg No	Phone No / Mobile No	Email Address

Nature Of Work Undertaken	Location / Area Of Work

Date	Contractor Time In	Contractor Time Out	Signature

Date	Keys/Key Fobs Time Out	Keys/Key Fobs Time In	Signature

Date Work Started	Time Work Started	Date Work Completed	Time Work Completed

Work Checked By	Date	Time

Important Notes	

Log/Reference No	Badge No	Authorised By	Date

Contractors Name	Contractors Company Name

Vehicle Reg No	Phone No / Mobile No	Email Address

Nature Of Work Undertaken	Location / Area Of Work

Date	Contractor Time In	Contractor Time Out	Signature

Date	Keys/Key Fobs Time Out	Keys/Key Fobs Time In	Signature

Date Work Started	Time Work Started	Date Work Completed	Time Work Completed

Work Checked By	Date	Time

Important Notes	

Log/Reference No	Badge No	Authorised By	Date

Contractors Name		Contractors Company Name	

Vehicle Reg No	Phone No / Mobile No	Email Address

Nature Of Work Undertaken		Location / Area Of Work	

Date	Contractor Time In	Contractor Time Out	Signature

Date	Keys/Key Fobs Time Out	Keys/Key Fobs Time In	Signature

Date Work Started	Time Work Started	Date Work Completed	Time Work Completed

Work Checked By		Date	Time

Important Notes	

Log/Reference No	Badge No	Authorised By	Date

Contractors Name		Contractors Company Name	

Vehicle Reg No	Phone No / Mobile No	Email Address

Nature Of Work Undertaken		Location / Area Of Work	

Date	Contractor Time In	Contractor Time Out	Signature

Date	Keys/Key Fobs Time Out	Keys/Key Fobs Time In	Signature

Date Work Started	Time Work Started	Date Work Completed	Time Work Completed

Work Checked By		Date	Time

Important Notes	

Log/Reference No	Badge No	Authorised By	Date

Contractors Name	Contractors Company Name

Vehicle Reg No	Phone No / Mobile No	Email Address

Nature Of Work Undertaken	Location / Area Of Work

Date	Contractor Time In	Contractor Time Out	Signature

Date	Keys/Key Fobs Time Out	Keys/Key Fobs Time In	Signature

Date Work Started	Time Work Started	Date Work Completed	Time Work Completed

Work Checked By	Date	Time

Important Notes	

Log/Reference No	Badge No	Authorised By	Date

Contractors Name	Contractors Company Name

Vehicle Reg No	Phone No / Mobile No	Email Address

Nature Of Work Undertaken	Location / Area Of Work

Date	Contractor Time In	Contractor Time Out	Signature

Date	Keys/Key Fobs Time Out	Keys/Key Fobs Time In	Signature

Date Work Started	Time Work Started	Date Work Completed	Time Work Completed

Work Checked By	Date	Time

Important Notes	

Log/Reference No	Badge No	Authorised By	Date

Contractors Name	Contractors Company Name

Vehicle Reg No	Phone No / Mobile No	Email Address

Nature Of Work Undertaken	Location / Area Of Work

Date	Contractor Time In	Contractor Time Out	Signature

Date	Keys/Key Fobs Time Out	Keys/Key Fobs Time In	Signature

Date Work Started	Time Work Started	Date Work Completed	Time Work Completed

Work Checked By	Date	Time

Important Notes	

Log/Reference No	Badge No	Authorised By	Date

Contractors Name	Contractors Company Name

Vehicle Reg No	Phone No / Mobile No	Email Address

Nature Of Work Undertaken	Location / Area Of Work

Date	Contractor Time In	Contractor Time Out	Signature

Date	Keys/Key Fobs Time Out	Keys/Key Fobs Time In	Signature

Date Work Started	Time Work Started	Date Work Completed	Time Work Completed

Work Checked By	Date	Time

Important Notes	

Log/Reference No	Badge No	Authorised By	Date

Contractors Name		Contractors Company Name	

Vehicle Reg No	Phone No / Mobile No	Email Address

Nature Of Work Undertaken		Location / Area Of Work	

Date	Contractor Time In	Contractor Time Out	Signature

Date	Keys/Key Fobs Time Out	Keys/Key Fobs Time In	Signature

Date Work Started	Time Work Started	Date Work Completed	Time Work Completed

Work Checked By		Date	Time

Important Notes	

Log/Reference No	Badge No	Authorised By	Date

Contractors Name		Contractors Company Name	

Vehicle Reg No	Phone No / Mobile No	Email Address

Nature Of Work Undertaken		Location / Area Of Work	

Date	Contractor Time In	Contractor Time Out	Signature

Date	Keys/Key Fobs Time Out	Keys/Key Fobs Time In	Signature

Date Work Started	Time Work Started	Date Work Completed	Time Work Completed

Work Checked By		Date	Time

Important Notes	

Log/Reference No	Badge No	Authorised By	Date

Contractors Name		Contractors Company Name	

Vehicle Reg No	Phone No / Mobile No		Email Address

Nature Of Work Undertaken		Location / Area Of Work	

Date	Contractor Time In	Contractor Time Out	Signature

Date	Keys/Key Fobs Time Out	Keys/Key Fobs Time In	Signature

Date Work Started	Time Work Started	Date Work Completed	Time Work Completed

Work Checked By		Date	Time

Important Notes	

Log/Reference No	Badge No	Authorised By	Date

Contractors Name		Contractors Company Name	

Vehicle Reg No	Phone No / Mobile No		Email Address

Nature Of Work Undertaken		Location / Area Of Work	

Date	Contractor Time In	Contractor Time Out	Signature

Date	Keys/Key Fobs Time Out	Keys/Key Fobs Time In	Signature

Date Work Started	Time Work Started	Date Work Completed	Time Work Completed

Work Checked By		Date	Time

Important Notes	

Log/Reference No	Badge No	Authorised By	Date

Contractors Name	Contractors Company Name

Vehicle Reg No	Phone No / Mobile No	Email Address

Nature Of Work Undertaken	Location / Area Of Work

Date	Contractor Time In	Contractor Time Out	Signature

Date	Keys/Key Fobs Time Out	Keys/Key Fobs Time In	Signature

Date Work Started	Time Work Started	Date Work Completed	Time Work Completed

Work Checked By	Date	Time

Important Notes	

Log/Reference No	Badge No	Authorised By	Date

Contractors Name	Contractors Company Name

Vehicle Reg No	Phone No / Mobile No	Email Address

Nature Of Work Undertaken	Location / Area Of Work

Date	Contractor Time In	Contractor Time Out	Signature

Date	Keys/Key Fobs Time Out	Keys/Key Fobs Time In	Signature

Date Work Started	Time Work Started	Date Work Completed	Time Work Completed

Work Checked By	Date	Time

Important Notes	

Log/Reference No	Badge No	Authorised By	Date

Contractors Name	Contractors Company Name

Vehicle Reg No	Phone No / Mobile No	Email Address

Nature Of Work Undertaken	Location / Area Of Work

Date	Contractor Time In	Contractor Time Out	Signature

Date	Keys/Key Fobs Time Out	Keys/Key Fobs Time In	Signature

Date Work Started	Time Work Started	Date Work Completed	Time Work Completed

Work Checked By	Date	Time

Important Notes	

Log/Reference No	Badge No	Authorised By	Date

Contractors Name	Contractors Company Name

Vehicle Reg No	Phone No / Mobile No	Email Address

Nature Of Work Undertaken	Location / Area Of Work

Date	Contractor Time In	Contractor Time Out	Signature

Date	Keys/Key Fobs Time Out	Keys/Key Fobs Time In	Signature

Date Work Started	Time Work Started	Date Work Completed	Time Work Completed

Work Checked By	Date	Time

Important Notes	

Log/Reference No	Badge No	Authorised By	Date

Contractors Name		Contractors Company Name	

Vehicle Reg No	Phone No / Mobile No	Email Address	

Nature Of Work Undertaken		Location / Area Of Work	

Date	Contractor Time In	Contractor Time Out	Signature

Date	Keys/Key Fobs Time Out	Keys/Key Fobs Time In	Signature

Date Work Started	Time Work Started	Date Work Completed	Time Work Completed

Work Checked By		Date	Time

Important Notes	

Log/Reference No	Badge No	Authorised By	Date

Contractors Name		Contractors Company Name	

Vehicle Reg No	Phone No / Mobile No	Email Address	

Nature Of Work Undertaken		Location / Area Of Work	

Date	Contractor Time In	Contractor Time Out	Signature

Date	Keys/Key Fobs Time Out	Keys/Key Fobs Time In	Signature

Date Work Started	Time Work Started	Date Work Completed	Time Work Completed

Work Checked By		Date	Time

Important Notes	

Log/Reference No		Badge No		Authorised By		Date	

Contractors Name		Contractors Company Name	

Vehicle Reg No		Phone No / Mobile No		Email Address	

Nature Of Work Undertaken		Location / Area Of Work	

Date	Contractor Time In	Contractor Time Out	Signature

Date	Keys/Key Fobs Time Out	Keys/Key Fobs Time In	Signature

Date Work Started	Time Work Started	Date Work Completed	Time Work Completed

Work Checked By		Date	Time

Important Notes	

Log/Reference No		Badge No		Authorised By		Date	

Contractors Name		Contractors Company Name	

Vehicle Reg No		Phone No / Mobile No		Email Address	

Nature Of Work Undertaken		Location / Area Of Work	

Date	Contractor Time In	Contractor Time Out	Signature

Date	Keys/Key Fobs Time Out	Keys/Key Fobs Time In	Signature

Date Work Started	Time Work Started	Date Work Completed	Time Work Completed

Work Checked By		Date	Time

Important Notes	

Log/Reference No	Badge No	Authorised By	Date

Contractors Name	Contractors Company Name

Vehicle Reg No	Phone No / Mobile No	Email Address

Nature Of Work Undertaken	Location / Area Of Work

Date	Contractor Time In	Contractor Time Out	Signature

Date	Keys/Key Fobs Time Out	Keys/Key Fobs Time In	Signature

Date Work Started	Time Work Started	Date Work Completed	Time Work Completed

Work Checked By	Date	Time

Important Notes	

Log/Reference No	Badge No	Authorised By	Date

Contractors Name	Contractors Company Name

Vehicle Reg No	Phone No / Mobile No	Email Address

Nature Of Work Undertaken	Location / Area Of Work

Date	Contractor Time In	Contractor Time Out	Signature

Date	Keys/Key Fobs Time Out	Keys/Key Fobs Time In	Signature

Date Work Started	Time Work Started	Date Work Completed	Time Work Completed

Work Checked By	Date	Time

Important Notes	

Log/Reference No	Badge No	Authorised By	Date

Contractors Name	Contractors Company Name

Vehicle Reg No	Phone No / Mobile No	Email Address

Nature Of Work Undertaken	Location / Area Of Work

Date	Contractor Time In	Contractor Time Out	Signature

Date	Keys/Key Fobs Time Out	Keys/Key Fobs Time In	Signature

Date Work Started	Time Work Started	Date Work Completed	Time Work Completed

Work Checked By	Date	Time

Important Notes	

Log/Reference No	Badge No	Authorised By	Date

Contractors Name	Contractors Company Name

Vehicle Reg No	Phone No / Mobile No	Email Address

Nature Of Work Undertaken	Location / Area Of Work

Date	Contractor Time In	Contractor Time Out	Signature

Date	Keys/Key Fobs Time Out	Keys/Key Fobs Time In	Signature

Date Work Started	Time Work Started	Date Work Completed	Time Work Completed

Work Checked By	Date	Time

Important Notes	

Log/Reference No	Badge No	Authorised By	Date

Contractors Name	Contractors Company Name

Vehicle Reg No	Phone No / Mobile No	Email Address

Nature Of Work Undertaken	Location / Area Of Work

Date	Contractor Time In	Contractor Time Out	Signature

Date	Keys/Key Fobs Time Out	Keys/Key Fobs Time In	Signature

Date Work Started	Time Work Started	Date Work Completed	Time Work Completed

Work Checked By	Date	Time

Important Notes	

Log/Reference No	Badge No	Authorised By	Date

Contractors Name	Contractors Company Name

Vehicle Reg No	Phone No / Mobile No	Email Address

Nature Of Work Undertaken	Location / Area Of Work

Date	Contractor Time In	Contractor Time Out	Signature

Date	Keys/Key Fobs Time Out	Keys/Key Fobs Time In	Signature

Date Work Started	Time Work Started	Date Work Completed	Time Work Completed

Work Checked By	Date	Time

Important Notes	

Log/Reference No	Badge No	Authorised By	Date

Contractors Name	Contractors Company Name

Vehicle Reg No	Phone No / Mobile No	Email Address

Nature Of Work Undertaken	Location / Area Of Work

Date	Contractor Time In	Contractor Time Out	Signature

Date	Keys/Key Fobs Time Out	Keys/Key Fobs Time In	Signature

Date Work Started	Time Work Started	Date Work Completed	Time Work Completed

Work Checked By	Date	Time

Important Notes	

Log/Reference No	Badge No	Authorised By	Date

Contractors Name	Contractors Company Name

Vehicle Reg No	Phone No / Mobile No	Email Address

Nature Of Work Undertaken	Location / Area Of Work

Date	Contractor Time In	Contractor Time Out	Signature

Date	Keys/Key Fobs Time Out	Keys/Key Fobs Time In	Signature

Date Work Started	Time Work Started	Date Work Completed	Time Work Completed

Work Checked By	Date	Time

Important Notes	

Log/Reference No	Badge No	Authorised By	Date

Contractors Name	Contractors Company Name

Vehicle Reg No	Phone No / Mobile No	Email Address

Nature Of Work Undertaken	Location / Area Of Work

Date	Contractor Time In	Contractor Time Out	Signature

Date	Keys/Key Fobs Time Out	Keys/Key Fobs Time In	Signature

Date Work Started	Time Work Started	Date Work Completed	Time Work Completed

Work Checked By	Date	Time

Important Notes	

Log/Reference No	Badge No	Authorised By	Date

Contractors Name	Contractors Company Name

Vehicle Reg No	Phone No / Mobile No	Email Address

Nature Of Work Undertaken	Location / Area Of Work

Date	Contractor Time In	Contractor Time Out	Signature

Date	Keys/Key Fobs Time Out	Keys/Key Fobs Time In	Signature

Date Work Started	Time Work Started	Date Work Completed	Time Work Completed

Work Checked By	Date	Time

Important Notes	

Log/Reference No	Badge No	Authorised By	Date

Contractors Name	Contractors Company Name

Vehicle Reg No	Phone No / Mobile No	Email Address

Nature Of Work Undertaken	Location / Area Of Work

Date	Contractor Time In	Contractor Time Out	Signature

Date	Keys/Key Fobs Time Out	Keys/Key Fobs Time In	Signature

Date Work Started	Time Work Started	Date Work Completed	Time Work Completed

Work Checked By	Date	Time

Important Notes	

Log/Reference No	Badge No	Authorised By	Date

Contractors Name	Contractors Company Name

Vehicle Reg No	Phone No / Mobile No	Email Address

Nature Of Work Undertaken	Location / Area Of Work

Date	Contractor Time In	Contractor Time Out	Signature

Date	Keys/Key Fobs Time Out	Keys/Key Fobs Time In	Signature

Date Work Started	Time Work Started	Date Work Completed	Time Work Completed

Work Checked By	Date	Time

Important Notes	

Log/Reference No	Badge No	Authorised By	Date

Contractors Name	Contractors Company Name

Vehicle Reg No	Phone No / Mobile No	Email Address

Nature Of Work Undertaken	Location / Area Of Work

Date	Contractor Time In	Contractor Time Out	Signature

Date	Keys/Key Fobs Time Out	Keys/Key Fobs Time In	Signature

Date Work Started	Time Work Started	Date Work Completed	Time Work Completed

Work Checked By	Date	Time

Important Notes	

Log/Reference No	Badge No	Authorised By	Date

Contractors Name	Contractors Company Name

Vehicle Reg No	Phone No / Mobile No	Email Address

Nature Of Work Undertaken	Location / Area Of Work

Date	Contractor Time In	Contractor Time Out	Signature

Date	Keys/Key Fobs Time Out	Keys/Key Fobs Time In	Signature

Date Work Started	Time Work Started	Date Work Completed	Time Work Completed

Work Checked By	Date	Time

Important Notes	

Log/Reference No	Badge No	Authorised By	Date

Contractors Name		Contractors Company Name	

Vehicle Reg No		Phone No / Mobile No	Email Address

Nature Of Work Undertaken		Location / Area Of Work	

Date	Contractor Time In	Contractor Time Out	Signature

Date	Keys/Key Fobs Time Out	Keys/Key Fobs Time In	Signature

Date Work Started	Time Work Started	Date Work Completed	Time Work Completed

Work Checked By		Date	Time

Important Notes	

Log/Reference No	Badge No	Authorised By	Date

Contractors Name		Contractors Company Name	

Vehicle Reg No		Phone No / Mobile No	Email Address

Nature Of Work Undertaken		Location / Area Of Work	

Date	Contractor Time In	Contractor Time Out	Signature

Date	Keys/Key Fobs Time Out	Keys/Key Fobs Time In	Signature

Date Work Started	Time Work Started	Date Work Completed	Time Work Completed

Work Checked By		Date	Time

Important Notes	

Log/Reference No	Badge No	Authorised By	Date

Contractors Name		Contractors Company Name	

Vehicle Reg No	Phone No / Mobile No	Email Address

Nature Of Work Undertaken		Location / Area Of Work	

Date	Contractor Time In	Contractor Time Out	Signature

Date	Keys/Key Fobs Time Out	Keys/Key Fobs Time In	Signature

Date Work Started	Time Work Started	Date Work Completed	Time Work Completed

Work Checked By		Date	Time

Important Notes	

Log/Reference No	Badge No	Authorised By	Date

Contractors Name		Contractors Company Name	

Vehicle Reg No	Phone No / Mobile No	Email Address

Nature Of Work Undertaken		Location / Area Of Work	

Date	Contractor Time In	Contractor Time Out	Signature

Date	Keys/Key Fobs Time Out	Keys/Key Fobs Time In	Signature

Date Work Started	Time Work Started	Date Work Completed	Time Work Completed

Work Checked By		Date	Time

Important Notes	

Log/Reference No	Badge No	Authorised By	Date

Contractors Name	Contractors Company Name

Vehicle Reg No	Phone No / Mobile No	Email Address

Nature Of Work Undertaken	Location / Area Of Work

Date	Contractor Time In	Contractor Time Out	Signature

Date	Keys/Key Fobs Time Out	Keys/Key Fobs Time In	Signature

Date Work Started	Time Work Started	Date Work Completed	Time Work Completed

Work Checked By	Date	Time

Important Notes	

Log/Reference No	Badge No	Authorised By	Date

Contractors Name	Contractors Company Name

Vehicle Reg No	Phone No / Mobile No	Email Address

Nature Of Work Undertaken	Location / Area Of Work

Date	Contractor Time In	Contractor Time Out	Signature

Date	Keys/Key Fobs Time Out	Keys/Key Fobs Time In	Signature

Date Work Started	Time Work Started	Date Work Completed	Time Work Completed

Work Checked By	Date	Time

Important Notes	

Log/Reference No	Badge No	Authorised By	Date

Contractors Name	Contractors Company Name

Vehicle Reg No	Phone No / Mobile No	Email Address

Nature Of Work Undertaken	Location / Area Of Work

Date	Contractor Time In	Contractor Time Out	Signature

Date	Keys/Key Fobs Time Out	Keys/Key Fobs Time In	Signature

Date Work Started	Time Work Started	Date Work Completed	Time Work Completed

Work Checked By	Date	Time

Important Notes	

Log/Reference No	Badge No	Authorised By	Date

Contractors Name	Contractors Company Name

Vehicle Reg No	Phone No / Mobile No	Email Address

Nature Of Work Undertaken	Location / Area Of Work

Date	Contractor Time In	Contractor Time Out	Signature

Date	Keys/Key Fobs Time Out	Keys/Key Fobs Time In	Signature

Date Work Started	Time Work Started	Date Work Completed	Time Work Completed

Work Checked By	Date	Time

Important Notes	

Log/Reference No	Badge No	Authorised By	Date

Contractors Name	Contractors Company Name

Vehicle Reg No	Phone No / Mobile No	Email Address

Nature Of Work Undertaken	Location / Area Of Work

Date	Contractor Time In	Contractor Time Out	Signature

Date	Keys/Key Fobs Time Out	Keys/Key Fobs Time In	Signature

Date Work Started	Time Work Started	Date Work Completed	Time Work Completed

Work Checked By	Date	Time

Important Notes	

Log/Reference No	Badge No	Authorised By	Date

Contractors Name	Contractors Company Name

Vehicle Reg No	Phone No / Mobile No	Email Address

Nature Of Work Undertaken	Location / Area Of Work

Date	Contractor Time In	Contractor Time Out	Signature

Date	Keys/Key Fobs Time Out	Keys/Key Fobs Time In	Signature

Date Work Started	Time Work Started	Date Work Completed	Time Work Completed

Work Checked By	Date	Time

Important Notes	

Log/Reference No	Badge No	Authorised By	Date

Contractors Name		Contractors Company Name	

Vehicle Reg No	Phone No / Mobile No		Email Address

Nature Of Work Undertaken		Location / Area Of Work	

Date	Contractor Time In	Contractor Time Out	Signature

Date	Keys/Key Fobs Time Out	Keys/Key Fobs Time In	Signature

Date Work Started	Time Work Started	Date Work Completed	Time Work Completed

Work Checked By		Date	Time

Important Notes	

Log/Reference No	Badge No	Authorised By	Date

Contractors Name		Contractors Company Name	

Vehicle Reg No	Phone No / Mobile No		Email Address

Nature Of Work Undertaken		Location / Area Of Work	

Date	Contractor Time In	Contractor Time Out	Signature

Date	Keys/Key Fobs Time Out	Keys/Key Fobs Time In	Signature

Date Work Started	Time Work Started	Date Work Completed	Time Work Completed

Work Checked By		Date	Time

Important Notes	

Log/Reference No	Badge No	Authorised By	Date

Contractors Name	Contractors Company Name

Vehicle Reg No	Phone No / Mobile No	Email Address

Nature Of Work Undertaken	Location / Area Of Work

Date	Contractor Time In	Contractor Time Out	Signature

Date	Keys/Key Fobs Time Out	Keys/Key Fobs Time In	Signature

Date Work Started	Time Work Started	Date Work Completed	Time Work Completed

Work Checked By	Date	Time

Important Notes	

Log/Reference No	Badge No	Authorised By	Date

Contractors Name	Contractors Company Name

Vehicle Reg No	Phone No / Mobile No	Email Address

Nature Of Work Undertaken	Location / Area Of Work

Date	Contractor Time In	Contractor Time Out	Signature

Date	Keys/Key Fobs Time Out	Keys/Key Fobs Time In	Signature

Date Work Started	Time Work Started	Date Work Completed	Time Work Completed

Work Checked By	Date	Time

Important Notes	

Log/Reference No	Badge No	Authorised By	Date

Contractors Name	Contractors Company Name

Vehicle Reg No	Phone No / Mobile No	Email Address

Nature Of Work Undertaken	Location / Area Of Work

Date	Contractor Time In	Contractor Time Out	Signature

Date	Keys/Key Fobs Time Out	Keys/Key Fobs Time In	Signature

Date Work Started	Time Work Started	Date Work Completed	Time Work Completed

Work Checked By	Date	Time

Important Notes	

Log/Reference No	Badge No	Authorised By	Date

Contractors Name	Contractors Company Name

Vehicle Reg No	Phone No / Mobile No	Email Address

Nature Of Work Undertaken	Location / Area Of Work

Date	Contractor Time In	Contractor Time Out	Signature

Date	Keys/Key Fobs Time Out	Keys/Key Fobs Time In	Signature

Date Work Started	Time Work Started	Date Work Completed	Time Work Completed

Work Checked By	Date	Time

Important Notes	

Log/Reference No	Badge No	Authorised By	Date

Contractors Name		Contractors Company Name	

Vehicle Reg No	Phone No / Mobile No	Email Address

Nature Of Work Undertaken		Location / Area Of Work	

Date	Contractor Time In	Contractor Time Out	Signature

Date	Keys/Key Fobs Time Out	Keys/Key Fobs Time In	Signature

Date Work Started	Time Work Started	Date Work Completed	Time Work Completed

Work Checked By		Date	Time

Important Notes	

Log/Reference No	Badge No	Authorised By	Date

Contractors Name		Contractors Company Name	

Vehicle Reg No	Phone No / Mobile No	Email Address

Nature Of Work Undertaken		Location / Area Of Work	

Date	Contractor Time In	Contractor Time Out	Signature

Date	Keys/Key Fobs Time Out	Keys/Key Fobs Time In	Signature

Date Work Started	Time Work Started	Date Work Completed	Time Work Completed

Work Checked By		Date	Time

Important Notes	

Log/Reference No	Badge No	Authorised By	Date

Contractors Name	Contractors Company Name

Vehicle Reg No	Phone No / Mobile No	Email Address

Nature Of Work Undertaken	Location / Area Of Work

Date	Contractor Time In	Contractor Time Out	Signature

Date	Keys/Key Fobs Time Out	Keys/Key Fobs Time In	Signature

Date Work Started	Time Work Started	Date Work Completed	Time Work Completed

Work Checked By	Date	Time

Important Notes	

Log/Reference No	Badge No	Authorised By	Date

Contractors Name	Contractors Company Name

Vehicle Reg No	Phone No / Mobile No	Email Address

Nature Of Work Undertaken	Location / Area Of Work

Date	Contractor Time In	Contractor Time Out	Signature

Date	Keys/Key Fobs Time Out	Keys/Key Fobs Time In	Signature

Date Work Started	Time Work Started	Date Work Completed	Time Work Completed

Work Checked By	Date	Time

Important Notes	

Log/Reference No		Badge No		Authorised By		Date	

Contractors Name		Contractors Company Name	

Vehicle Reg No		Phone No / Mobile No		Email Address	

Nature Of Work Undertaken		Location / Area Of Work	

Date	Contractor Time In	Contractor Time Out	Signature

Date	Keys/Key Fobs Time Out	Keys/Key Fobs Time In	Signature

Date Work Started	Time Work Started	Date Work Completed	Time Work Completed

Work Checked By		Date	Time

Important Notes	

Log/Reference No		Badge No		Authorised By		Date	

Contractors Name		Contractors Company Name	

Vehicle Reg No		Phone No / Mobile No		Email Address	

Nature Of Work Undertaken		Location / Area Of Work	

Date	Contractor Time In	Contractor Time Out	Signature

Date	Keys/Key Fobs Time Out	Keys/Key Fobs Time In	Signature

Date Work Started	Time Work Started	Date Work Completed	Time Work Completed

Work Checked By		Date	Time

Important Notes	

Log/Reference No	Badge No	Authorised By	Date

Contractors Name	Contractors Company Name

Vehicle Reg No	Phone No / Mobile No	Email Address

Nature Of Work Undertaken	Location / Area Of Work

Date	Contractor Time In	Contractor Time Out	Signature

Date	Keys/Key Fobs Time Out	Keys/Key Fobs Time In	Signature

Date Work Started	Time Work Started	Date Work Completed	Time Work Completed

Work Checked By	Date	Time

Important Notes	

Log/Reference No	Badge No	Authorised By	Date

Contractors Name	Contractors Company Name

Vehicle Reg No	Phone No / Mobile No	Email Address

Nature Of Work Undertaken	Location / Area Of Work

Date	Contractor Time In	Contractor Time Out	Signature

Date	Keys/Key Fobs Time Out	Keys/Key Fobs Time In	Signature

Date Work Started	Time Work Started	Date Work Completed	Time Work Completed

Work Checked By	Date	Time

Important Notes	

Log/Reference No	Badge No	Authorised By	Date

Contractors Name		Contractors Company Name	

Vehicle Reg No	Phone No / Mobile No	Email Address

Nature Of Work Undertaken		Location / Area Of Work	

Date	Contractor Time In	Contractor Time Out	Signature

Date	Keys/Key Fobs Time Out	Keys/Key Fobs Time In	Signature

Date Work Started	Time Work Started	Date Work Completed	Time Work Completed

Work Checked By		Date	Time

Important Notes	

Log/Reference No	Badge No	Authorised By	Date

Contractors Name		Contractors Company Name	

Vehicle Reg No	Phone No / Mobile No	Email Address

Nature Of Work Undertaken		Location / Area Of Work	

Date	Contractor Time In	Contractor Time Out	Signature

Date	Keys/Key Fobs Time Out	Keys/Key Fobs Time In	Signature

Date Work Started	Time Work Started	Date Work Completed	Time Work Completed

Work Checked By		Date	Time

Important Notes	

Log/Reference No	Badge No	Authorised By	Date

Contractors Name	Contractors Company Name

Vehicle Reg No	Phone No / Mobile No	Email Address

Nature Of Work Undertaken	Location / Area Of Work

Date	Contractor Time In	Contractor Time Out	Signature

Date	Keys/Key Fobs Time Out	Keys/Key Fobs Time In	Signature

Date Work Started	Time Work Started	Date Work Completed	Time Work Completed

Work Checked By	Date	Time

Important Notes	

Log/Reference No	Badge No	Authorised By	Date

Contractors Name	Contractors Company Name

Vehicle Reg No	Phone No / Mobile No	Email Address

Nature Of Work Undertaken	Location / Area Of Work

Date	Contractor Time In	Contractor Time Out	Signature

Date	Keys/Key Fobs Time Out	Keys/Key Fobs Time In	Signature

Date Work Started	Time Work Started	Date Work Completed	Time Work Completed

Work Checked By	Date	Time

Important Notes	

Log/Reference No	Badge No	Authorised By	Date

Contractors Name	Contractors Company Name

Vehicle Reg No	Phone No / Mobile No	Email Address

Nature Of Work Undertaken	Location / Area Of Work

Date	Contractor Time In	Contractor Time Out	Signature

Date	Keys/Key Fobs Time Out	Keys/Key Fobs Time In	Signature

Date Work Started	Time Work Started	Date Work Completed	Time Work Completed

Work Checked By	Date	Time

Important Notes	

Log/Reference No	Badge No	Authorised By	Date

Contractors Name	Contractors Company Name

Vehicle Reg No	Phone No / Mobile No	Email Address

Nature Of Work Undertaken	Location / Area Of Work

Date	Contractor Time In	Contractor Time Out	Signature

Date	Keys/Key Fobs Time Out	Keys/Key Fobs Time In	Signature

Date Work Started	Time Work Started	Date Work Completed	Time Work Completed

Work Checked By	Date	Time

Important Notes	

Log/Reference No	Badge No	Authorised By	Date

Contractors Name		Contractors Company Name	

Vehicle Reg No	Phone No / Mobile No	Email Address	

Nature Of Work Undertaken		Location / Area Of Work	

Date	Contractor Time In	Contractor Time Out	Signature

Date	Keys/Key Fobs Time Out	Keys/Key Fobs Time In	Signature

Date Work Started	Time Work Started	Date Work Completed	Time Work Completed

Work Checked By		Date	Time

Important Notes	

Log/Reference No	Badge No	Authorised By	Date

Contractors Name		Contractors Company Name	

Vehicle Reg No	Phone No / Mobile No	Email Address	

Nature Of Work Undertaken		Location / Area Of Work	

Date	Contractor Time In	Contractor Time Out	Signature

Date	Keys/Key Fobs Time Out	Keys/Key Fobs Time In	Signature

Date Work Started	Time Work Started	Date Work Completed	Time Work Completed

Work Checked By		Date	Time

Important Notes	

Log/Reference No	Badge No	Authorised By	Date

Contractors Name	Contractors Company Name

Vehicle Reg No	Phone No / Mobile No	Email Address

Nature Of Work Undertaken	Location / Area Of Work

Date	Contractor Time In	Contractor Time Out	Signature

Date	Keys/Key Fobs Time Out	Keys/Key Fobs Time In	Signature

Date Work Started	Time Work Started	Date Work Completed	Time Work Completed

Work Checked By	Date	Time

Important Notes	

Log/Reference No	Badge No	Authorised By	Date

Contractors Name	Contractors Company Name

Vehicle Reg No	Phone No / Mobile No	Email Address

Nature Of Work Undertaken	Location / Area Of Work

Date	Contractor Time In	Contractor Time Out	Signature

Date	Keys/Key Fobs Time Out	Keys/Key Fobs Time In	Signature

Date Work Started	Time Work Started	Date Work Completed	Time Work Completed

Work Checked By	Date	Time

Important Notes	

Log/Reference No	Badge No	Authorised By	Date

Contractors Name	Contractors Company Name

Vehicle Reg No	Phone No / Mobile No	Email Address

Nature Of Work Undertaken	Location / Area Of Work

Date	Contractor Time In	Contractor Time Out	Signature

Date	Keys/Key Fobs Time Out	Keys/Key Fobs Time In	Signature

Date Work Started	Time Work Started	Date Work Completed	Time Work Completed

Work Checked By	Date	Time

Important Notes	

Log/Reference No	Badge No	Authorised By	Date

Contractors Name	Contractors Company Name

Vehicle Reg No	Phone No / Mobile No	Email Address

Nature Of Work Undertaken	Location / Area Of Work

Date	Contractor Time In	Contractor Time Out	Signature

Date	Keys/Key Fobs Time Out	Keys/Key Fobs Time In	Signature

Date Work Started	Time Work Started	Date Work Completed	Time Work Completed

Work Checked By	Date	Time

Important Notes	

Log/Reference No	Badge No	Authorised By	Date

Contractors Name	Contractors Company Name

Vehicle Reg No	Phone No / Mobile No	Email Address

Nature Of Work Undertaken	Location / Area Of Work

Date	Contractor Time In	Contractor Time Out	Signature

Date	Keys/Key Fobs Time Out	Keys/Key Fobs Time In	Signature

Date Work Started	Time Work Started	Date Work Completed	Time Work Completed

Work Checked By	Date	Time

Important Notes	

Log/Reference No	Badge No	Authorised By	Date

Contractors Name	Contractors Company Name

Vehicle Reg No	Phone No / Mobile No	Email Address

Nature Of Work Undertaken	Location / Area Of Work

Date	Contractor Time In	Contractor Time Out	Signature

Date	Keys/Key Fobs Time Out	Keys/Key Fobs Time In	Signature

Date Work Started	Time Work Started	Date Work Completed	Time Work Completed

Work Checked By	Date	Time

Important Notes	

Log/Reference No	Badge No	Authorised By	Date

Contractors Name		Contractors Company Name	

Vehicle Reg No	Phone No / Mobile No	Email Address

Nature Of Work Undertaken		Location / Area Of Work	

Date	Contractor Time In	Contractor Time Out	Signature

Date	Keys/Key Fobs Time Out	Keys/Key Fobs Time In	Signature

Date Work Started	Time Work Started	Date Work Completed	Time Work Completed

Work Checked By		Date	Time

Important Notes	

Log/Reference No	Badge No	Authorised By	Date

Contractors Name		Contractors Company Name	

Vehicle Reg No	Phone No / Mobile No	Email Address

Nature Of Work Undertaken		Location / Area Of Work	

Date	Contractor Time In	Contractor Time Out	Signature

Date	Keys/Key Fobs Time Out	Keys/Key Fobs Time In	Signature

Date Work Started	Time Work Started	Date Work Completed	Time Work Completed

Work Checked By		Date	Time

Important Notes	

Log/Reference No	Badge No	Authorised By	Date

Contractors Name		Contractors Company Name	

Vehicle Reg No	Phone No / Mobile No	Email Address

Nature Of Work Undertaken		Location / Area Of Work	

Date	Contractor Time In	Contractor Time Out	Signature

Date	Keys/Key Fobs Time Out	Keys/Key Fobs Time In	Signature

Date Work Started	Time Work Started	Date Work Completed	Time Work Completed

Work Checked By		Date	Time

Important Notes	

Log/Reference No	Badge No	Authorised By	Date

Contractors Name		Contractors Company Name	

Vehicle Reg No	Phone No / Mobile No	Email Address

Nature Of Work Undertaken		Location / Area Of Work	

Date	Contractor Time In	Contractor Time Out	Signature

Date	Keys/Key Fobs Time Out	Keys/Key Fobs Time In	Signature

Date Work Started	Time Work Started	Date Work Completed	Time Work Completed

Work Checked By		Date	Time

Important Notes	

Log/Reference No	Badge No	Authorised By	Date

Contractors Name	Contractors Company Name

Vehicle Reg No	Phone No / Mobile No	Email Address

Nature Of Work Undertaken	Location / Area Of Work

Date	Contractor Time In	Contractor Time Out	Signature

Date	Keys/Key Fobs Time Out	Keys/Key Fobs Time In	Signature

Date Work Started	Time Work Started	Date Work Completed	Time Work Completed

Work Checked By	Date	Time

Important Notes	

Log/Reference No	Badge No	Authorised By	Date

Contractors Name	Contractors Company Name

Vehicle Reg No	Phone No / Mobile No	Email Address

Nature Of Work Undertaken	Location / Area Of Work

Date	Contractor Time In	Contractor Time Out	Signature

Date	Keys/Key Fobs Time Out	Keys/Key Fobs Time In	Signature

Date Work Started	Time Work Started	Date Work Completed	Time Work Completed

Work Checked By	Date	Time

Important Notes	

Log/Reference No	Badge No	Authorised By	Date

Contractors Name	Contractors Company Name

Vehicle Reg No	Phone No / Mobile No	Email Address

Nature Of Work Undertaken	Location / Area Of Work

Date	Contractor Time In	Contractor Time Out	Signature

Date	Keys/Key Fobs Time Out	Keys/Key Fobs Time In	Signature

Date Work Started	Time Work Started	Date Work Completed	Time Work Completed

Work Checked By	Date	Time

Important Notes	

Log/Reference No	Badge No	Authorised By	Date

Contractors Name	Contractors Company Name

Vehicle Reg No	Phone No / Mobile No	Email Address

Nature Of Work Undertaken	Location / Area Of Work

Date	Contractor Time In	Contractor Time Out	Signature

Date	Keys/Key Fobs Time Out	Keys/Key Fobs Time In	Signature

Date Work Started	Time Work Started	Date Work Completed	Time Work Completed

Work Checked By	Date	Time

Important Notes	

Log/Reference No	Badge No	Authorised By	Date

Contractors Name		Contractors Company Name	

Vehicle Reg No	Phone No / Mobile No		Email Address

Nature Of Work Undertaken		Location / Area Of Work	

Date	Contractor Time In	Contractor Time Out	Signature

Date	Keys/Key Fobs Time Out	Keys/Key Fobs Time In	Signature

Date Work Started	Time Work Started	Date Work Completed	Time Work Completed

Work Checked By		Date	Time

Important Notes	

Log/Reference No	Badge No	Authorised By	Date

Contractors Name		Contractors Company Name	

Vehicle Reg No	Phone No / Mobile No		Email Address

Nature Of Work Undertaken		Location / Area Of Work	

Date	Contractor Time In	Contractor Time Out	Signature

Date	Keys/Key Fobs Time Out	Keys/Key Fobs Time In	Signature

Date Work Started	Time Work Started	Date Work Completed	Time Work Completed

Work Checked By		Date	Time

Important Notes	

Log/Reference No	Badge No	Authorised By	Date

Contractors Name		Contractors Company Name	

Vehicle Reg No	Phone No / Mobile No	Email Address

Nature Of Work Undertaken	Location / Area Of Work

Date	Contractor Time In	Contractor Time Out	Signature

Date	Keys/Key Fobs Time Out	Keys/Key Fobs Time In	Signature

Date Work Started	Time Work Started	Date Work Completed	Time Work Completed

Work Checked By	Date	Time

Important Notes	

Log/Reference No	Badge No	Authorised By	Date

Contractors Name		Contractors Company Name	

Vehicle Reg No	Phone No / Mobile No	Email Address

Nature Of Work Undertaken	Location / Area Of Work

Date	Contractor Time In	Contractor Time Out	Signature

Date	Keys/Key Fobs Time Out	Keys/Key Fobs Time In	Signature

Date Work Started	Time Work Started	Date Work Completed	Time Work Completed

Work Checked By	Date	Time

Important Notes	

Log/Reference No	Badge No	Authorised By	Date

Contractors Name	Contractors Company Name

Vehicle Reg No	Phone No / Mobile No	Email Address

Nature Of Work Undertaken	Location / Area Of Work

Date	Contractor Time In	Contractor Time Out	Signature

Date	Keys/Key Fobs Time Out	Keys/Key Fobs Time In	Signature

Date Work Started	Time Work Started	Date Work Completed	Time Work Completed

Work Checked By	Date	Time

Important Notes	

Log/Reference No	Badge No	Authorised By	Date

Contractors Name	Contractors Company Name

Vehicle Reg No	Phone No / Mobile No	Email Address

Nature Of Work Undertaken	Location / Area Of Work

Date	Contractor Time In	Contractor Time Out	Signature

Date	Keys/Key Fobs Time Out	Keys/Key Fobs Time In	Signature

Date Work Started	Time Work Started	Date Work Completed	Time Work Completed

Work Checked By	Date	Time

Important Notes	

Log/Reference No		Badge No		Authorised By		Date	

Contractors Name			Contractors Company Name		

Vehicle Reg No		Phone No / Mobile No		Email Address	

Nature Of Work Undertaken			Location / Area Of Work		

Date	Contractor Time In	Contractor Time Out	Signature

Date	Keys/Key Fobs Time Out	Keys/Key Fobs Time In	Signature

Date Work Started	Time Work Started	Date Work Completed	Time Work Completed

Work Checked By		Date	Time

Important Notes	

Log/Reference No		Badge No		Authorised By		Date	

Contractors Name			Contractors Company Name		

Vehicle Reg No		Phone No / Mobile No		Email Address	

Nature Of Work Undertaken			Location / Area Of Work		

Date	Contractor Time In	Contractor Time Out	Signature

Date	Keys/Key Fobs Time Out	Keys/Key Fobs Time In	Signature

Date Work Started	Time Work Started	Date Work Completed	Time Work Completed

Work Checked By		Date	Time

Important Notes	

Log/Reference No	Badge No	Authorised By	Date

Contractors Name		Contractors Company Name	

Vehicle Reg No	Phone No / Mobile No	Email Address

Nature Of Work Undertaken		Location / Area Of Work	

Date	Contractor Time In	Contractor Time Out	Signature

Date	Keys/Key Fobs Time Out	Keys/Key Fobs Time In	Signature

Date Work Started	Time Work Started	Date Work Completed	Time Work Completed

Work Checked By		Date	Time

Important Notes	

Log/Reference No	Badge No	Authorised By	Date

Contractors Name		Contractors Company Name	

Vehicle Reg No	Phone No / Mobile No	Email Address

Nature Of Work Undertaken		Location / Area Of Work	

Date	Contractor Time In	Contractor Time Out	Signature

Date	Keys/Key Fobs Time Out	Keys/Key Fobs Time In	Signature

Date Work Started	Time Work Started	Date Work Completed	Time Work Completed

Work Checked By		Date	Time

Important Notes	

Log/Reference No	Badge No	Authorised By	Date

Contractors Name		Contractors Company Name	

Vehicle Reg No	Phone No / Mobile No	Email Address

Nature Of Work Undertaken		Location / Area Of Work	

Date	Contractor Time In	Contractor Time Out	Signature

Date	Keys/Key Fobs Time Out	Keys/Key Fobs Time In	Signature

Date Work Started	Time Work Started	Date Work Completed	Time Work Completed

Work Checked By		Date	Time

Important Notes	

Log/Reference No	Badge No	Authorised By	Date

Contractors Name		Contractors Company Name	

Vehicle Reg No	Phone No / Mobile No	Email Address

Nature Of Work Undertaken		Location / Area Of Work	

Date	Contractor Time In	Contractor Time Out	Signature

Date	Keys/Key Fobs Time Out	Keys/Key Fobs Time In	Signature

Date Work Started	Time Work Started	Date Work Completed	Time Work Completed

Work Checked By		Date	Time

Important Notes	

Log/Reference No	Badge No	Authorised By	Date

Contractors Name	Contractors Company Name

Vehicle Reg No	Phone No / Mobile No	Email Address

Nature Of Work Undertaken	Location / Area Of Work

Date	Contractor Time In	Contractor Time Out	Signature

Date	Keys/Key Fobs Time Out	Keys/Key Fobs Time In	Signature

Date Work Started	Time Work Started	Date Work Completed	Time Work Completed

Work Checked By	Date	Time

Important Notes	

Log/Reference No	Badge No	Authorised By	Date

Contractors Name	Contractors Company Name

Vehicle Reg No	Phone No / Mobile No	Email Address

Nature Of Work Undertaken	Location / Area Of Work

Date	Contractor Time In	Contractor Time Out	Signature

Date	Keys/Key Fobs Time Out	Keys/Key Fobs Time In	Signature

Date Work Started	Time Work Started	Date Work Completed	Time Work Completed

Work Checked By	Date	Time

Important Notes	

Log/Reference No	Badge No	Authorised By	Date

Contractors Name	Contractors Company Name

Vehicle Reg No	Phone No / Mobile No	Email Address

Nature Of Work Undertaken	Location / Area Of Work

Date	Contractor Time In	Contractor Time Out	Signature

Date	Keys/Key Fobs Time Out	Keys/Key Fobs Time In	Signature

Date Work Started	Time Work Started	Date Work Completed	Time Work Completed

Work Checked By	Date	Time

Important Notes	

Log/Reference No	Badge No	Authorised By	Date

Contractors Name	Contractors Company Name

Vehicle Reg No	Phone No / Mobile No	Email Address

Nature Of Work Undertaken	Location / Area Of Work

Date	Contractor Time In	Contractor Time Out	Signature

Date	Keys/Key Fobs Time Out	Keys/Key Fobs Time In	Signature

Date Work Started	Time Work Started	Date Work Completed	Time Work Completed

Work Checked By	Date	Time

Important Notes	

Log/Reference No	Badge No	Authorised By	Date

Contractors Name	Contractors Company Name

Vehicle Reg No	Phone No / Mobile No	Email Address

Nature Of Work Undertaken	Location / Area Of Work

Date	Contractor Time In	Contractor Time Out	Signature

Date	Keys/Key Fobs Time Out	Keys/Key Fobs Time In	Signature

Date Work Started	Time Work Started	Date Work Completed	Time Work Completed

Work Checked By	Date	Time

Important Notes	

Log/Reference No	Badge No	Authorised By	Date

Contractors Name	Contractors Company Name

Vehicle Reg No	Phone No / Mobile No	Email Address

Nature Of Work Undertaken	Location / Area Of Work

Date	Contractor Time In	Contractor Time Out	Signature

Date	Keys/Key Fobs Time Out	Keys/Key Fobs Time In	Signature

Date Work Started	Time Work Started	Date Work Completed	Time Work Completed

Work Checked By	Date	Time

Important Notes	

Log/Reference No	Badge No	Authorised By	Date

Contractors Name	Contractors Company Name

Vehicle Reg No	Phone No / Mobile No	Email Address

Nature Of Work Undertaken	Location / Area Of Work

Date	Contractor Time In	Contractor Time Out	Signature

Date	Keys/Key Fobs Time Out	Keys/Key Fobs Time In	Signature

Date Work Started	Time Work Started	Date Work Completed	Time Work Completed

Work Checked By	Date	Time

Important Notes	

Log/Reference No	Badge No	Authorised By	Date

Contractors Name	Contractors Company Name

Vehicle Reg No	Phone No / Mobile No	Email Address

Nature Of Work Undertaken	Location / Area Of Work

Date	Contractor Time In	Contractor Time Out	Signature

Date	Keys/Key Fobs Time Out	Keys/Key Fobs Time In	Signature

Date Work Started	Time Work Started	Date Work Completed	Time Work Completed

Work Checked By	Date	Time

Important Notes	

Log/Reference No	Badge No	Authorised By	Date

Contractors Name	Contractors Company Name

Vehicle Reg No	Phone No / Mobile No	Email Address

Nature Of Work Undertaken	Location / Area Of Work

Date	Contractor Time In	Contractor Time Out	Signature

Date	Keys/Key Fobs Time Out	Keys/Key Fobs Time In	Signature

Date Work Started	Time Work Started	Date Work Completed	Time Work Completed

Work Checked By	Date	Time

Important Notes	

Log/Reference No	Badge No	Authorised By	Date

Contractors Name	Contractors Company Name

Vehicle Reg No	Phone No / Mobile No	Email Address

Nature Of Work Undertaken	Location / Area Of Work

Date	Contractor Time In	Contractor Time Out	Signature

Date	Keys/Key Fobs Time Out	Keys/Key Fobs Time In	Signature

Date Work Started	Time Work Started	Date Work Completed	Time Work Completed

Work Checked By	Date	Time

Important Notes	

Log/Reference No	Badge No	Authorised By	Date

Contractors Name		Contractors Company Name	

Vehicle Reg No		Phone No / Mobile No		Email Address

Nature Of Work Undertaken		Location / Area Of Work	

Date	Contractor Time In	Contractor Time Out	Signature

Date	Keys/Key Fobs Time Out	Keys/Key Fobs Time In	Signature

Date Work Started	Time Work Started	Date Work Completed	Time Work Completed

Work Checked By		Date	Time

Important Notes	

Log/Reference No	Badge No	Authorised By	Date

Contractors Name		Contractors Company Name	

Vehicle Reg No		Phone No / Mobile No		Email Address

Nature Of Work Undertaken		Location / Area Of Work	

Date	Contractor Time In	Contractor Time Out	Signature

Date	Keys/Key Fobs Time Out	Keys/Key Fobs Time In	Signature

Date Work Started	Time Work Started	Date Work Completed	Time Work Completed

Work Checked By		Date	Time

Important Notes	

Log/Reference No	Badge No	Authorised By	Date

Contractors Name	Contractors Company Name

Vehicle Reg No	Phone No / Mobile No	Email Address

Nature Of Work Undertaken	Location / Area Of Work

Date	Contractor Time In	Contractor Time Out	Signature

Date	Keys/Key Fobs Time Out	Keys/Key Fobs Time In	Signature

Date Work Started	Time Work Started	Date Work Completed	Time Work Completed

Work Checked By	Date	Time

Important Notes	

Log/Reference No	Badge No	Authorised By	Date

Contractors Name	Contractors Company Name

Vehicle Reg No	Phone No / Mobile No	Email Address

Nature Of Work Undertaken	Location / Area Of Work

Date	Contractor Time In	Contractor Time Out	Signature

Date	Keys/Key Fobs Time Out	Keys/Key Fobs Time In	Signature

Date Work Started	Time Work Started	Date Work Completed	Time Work Completed

Work Checked By	Date	Time

Important Notes	

Log/Reference No	Badge No	Authorised By	Date

Contractors Name	Contractors Company Name

Vehicle Reg No	Phone No / Mobile No	Email Address

Nature Of Work Undertaken	Location / Area Of Work

Date	Contractor Time In	Contractor Time Out	Signature

Date	Keys/Key Fobs Time Out	Keys/Key Fobs Time In	Signature

Date Work Started	Time Work Started	Date Work Completed	Time Work Completed

Work Checked By	Date	Time

Important Notes	

Log/Reference No	Badge No	Authorised By	Date

Contractors Name	Contractors Company Name

Vehicle Reg No	Phone No / Mobile No	Email Address

Nature Of Work Undertaken	Location / Area Of Work

Date	Contractor Time In	Contractor Time Out	Signature

Date	Keys/Key Fobs Time Out	Keys/Key Fobs Time In	Signature

Date Work Started	Time Work Started	Date Work Completed	Time Work Completed

Work Checked By	Date	Time

Important Notes	

Log/Reference No	Badge No	Authorised By	Date

Contractors Name		Contractors Company Name	

Vehicle Reg No	Phone No / Mobile No	Email Address

Nature Of Work Undertaken		Location / Area Of Work	

Date	Contractor Time In	Contractor Time Out	Signature

Date	Keys/Key Fobs Time Out	Keys/Key Fobs Time In	Signature

Date Work Started	Time Work Started	Date Work Completed	Time Work Completed

Work Checked By		Date	Time

Important Notes	

Log/Reference No	Badge No	Authorised By	Date

Contractors Name		Contractors Company Name	

Vehicle Reg No	Phone No / Mobile No	Email Address

Nature Of Work Undertaken		Location / Area Of Work	

Date	Contractor Time In	Contractor Time Out	Signature

Date	Keys/Key Fobs Time Out	Keys/Key Fobs Time In	Signature

Date Work Started	Time Work Started	Date Work Completed	Time Work Completed

Work Checked By		Date	Time

Important Notes	

Log/Reference No	Badge No	Authorised By	Date

Contractors Name	Contractors Company Name

Vehicle Reg No	Phone No / Mobile No	Email Address

Nature Of Work Undertaken	Location / Area Of Work

Date	Contractor Time In	Contractor Time Out	Signature

Date	Keys/Key Fobs Time Out	Keys/Key Fobs Time In	Signature

Date Work Started	Time Work Started	Date Work Completed	Time Work Completed

Work Checked By	Date	Time

Important Notes	

Log/Reference No	Badge No	Authorised By	Date

Contractors Name	Contractors Company Name

Vehicle Reg No	Phone No / Mobile No	Email Address

Nature Of Work Undertaken	Location / Area Of Work

Date	Contractor Time In	Contractor Time Out	Signature

Date	Keys/Key Fobs Time Out	Keys/Key Fobs Time In	Signature

Date Work Started	Time Work Started	Date Work Completed	Time Work Completed

Work Checked By	Date	Time

Important Notes	

Log/Reference No	Badge No	Authorised By	Date

Contractors Name	Contractors Company Name

Vehicle Reg No	Phone No / Mobile No	Email Address

Nature Of Work Undertaken	Location / Area Of Work

Date	Contractor Time In	Contractor Time Out	Signature

Date	Keys/Key Fobs Time Out	Keys/Key Fobs Time In	Signature

Date Work Started	Time Work Started	Date Work Completed	Time Work Completed

Work Checked By	Date	Time

Important Notes	

Log/Reference No	Badge No	Authorised By	Date

Contractors Name	Contractors Company Name

Vehicle Reg No	Phone No / Mobile No	Email Address

Nature Of Work Undertaken	Location / Area Of Work

Date	Contractor Time In	Contractor Time Out	Signature

Date	Keys/Key Fobs Time Out	Keys/Key Fobs Time In	Signature

Date Work Started	Time Work Started	Date Work Completed	Time Work Completed

Work Checked By	Date	Time

Important Notes	

Log/Reference No	Badge No	Authorised By	Date

Contractors Name	Contractors Company Name

Vehicle Reg No	Phone No / Mobile No	Email Address

Nature Of Work Undertaken	Location / Area Of Work

Date	Contractor Time In	Contractor Time Out	Signature

Date	Keys/Key Fobs Time Out	Keys/Key Fobs Time In	Signature

Date Work Started	Time Work Started	Date Work Completed	Time Work Completed

Work Checked By	Date	Time

Important Notes	

Log/Reference No	Badge No	Authorised By	Date

Contractors Name	Contractors Company Name

Vehicle Reg No	Phone No / Mobile No	Email Address

Nature Of Work Undertaken	Location / Area Of Work

Date	Contractor Time In	Contractor Time Out	Signature

Date	Keys/Key Fobs Time Out	Keys/Key Fobs Time In	Signature

Date Work Started	Time Work Started	Date Work Completed	Time Work Completed

Work Checked By	Date	Time

Important Notes	

Log/Reference No	Badge No	Authorised By	Date

Contractors Name	Contractors Company Name

Vehicle Reg No	Phone No / Mobile No	Email Address

Nature Of Work Undertaken	Location / Area Of Work

Date	Contractor Time In	Contractor Time Out	Signature

Date	Keys/Key Fobs Time Out	Keys/Key Fobs Time In	Signature

Date Work Started	Time Work Started	Date Work Completed	Time Work Completed

Work Checked By	Date	Time

Important Notes	

Log/Reference No	Badge No	Authorised By	Date

Contractors Name	Contractors Company Name

Vehicle Reg No	Phone No / Mobile No	Email Address

Nature Of Work Undertaken	Location / Area Of Work

Date	Contractor Time In	Contractor Time Out	Signature

Date	Keys/Key Fobs Time Out	Keys/Key Fobs Time In	Signature

Date Work Started	Time Work Started	Date Work Completed	Time Work Completed

Work Checked By	Date	Time

Important Notes	

Log/Reference No	Badge No	Authorised By	Date

Contractors Name		Contractors Company Name	

Vehicle Reg No	Phone No / Mobile No	Email Address

Nature Of Work Undertaken		Location / Area Of Work	

Date	Contractor Time In	Contractor Time Out	Signature

Date	Keys/Key Fobs Time Out	Keys/Key Fobs Time In	Signature

Date Work Started	Time Work Started	Date Work Completed	Time Work Completed

Work Checked By		Date	Time

Important Notes	

Log/Reference No	Badge No	Authorised By	Date

Contractors Name		Contractors Company Name	

Vehicle Reg No	Phone No / Mobile No	Email Address

Nature Of Work Undertaken		Location / Area Of Work	

Date	Contractor Time In	Contractor Time Out	Signature

Date	Keys/Key Fobs Time Out	Keys/Key Fobs Time In	Signature

Date Work Started	Time Work Started	Date Work Completed	Time Work Completed

Work Checked By		Date	Time

Important Notes	

Log/Reference No	Badge No	Authorised By	Date

Contractors Name	Contractors Company Name

Vehicle Reg No	Phone No / Mobile No	Email Address

Nature Of Work Undertaken	Location / Area Of Work

Date	Contractor Time In	Contractor Time Out	Signature

Date	Keys/Key Fobs Time Out	Keys/Key Fobs Time In	Signature

Date Work Started	Time Work Started	Date Work Completed	Time Work Completed

Work Checked By	Date	Time

Important Notes	

Log/Reference No	Badge No	Authorised By	Date

Contractors Name	Contractors Company Name

Vehicle Reg No	Phone No / Mobile No	Email Address

Nature Of Work Undertaken	Location / Area Of Work

Date	Contractor Time In	Contractor Time Out	Signature

Date	Keys/Key Fobs Time Out	Keys/Key Fobs Time In	Signature

Date Work Started	Time Work Started	Date Work Completed	Time Work Completed

Work Checked By	Date	Time

Important Notes	

Log/Reference No	Badge No	Authorised By	Date

Contractors Name	Contractors Company Name

Vehicle Reg No	Phone No / Mobile No	Email Address

Nature Of Work Undertaken	Location / Area Of Work

Date	Contractor Time In	Contractor Time Out	Signature

Date	Keys/Key Fobs Time Out	Keys/Key Fobs Time In	Signature

Date Work Started	Time Work Started	Date Work Completed	Time Work Completed

Work Checked By	Date	Time

Important Notes	

Log/Reference No	Badge No	Authorised By	Date

Contractors Name	Contractors Company Name

Vehicle Reg No	Phone No / Mobile No	Email Address

Nature Of Work Undertaken	Location / Area Of Work

Date	Contractor Time In	Contractor Time Out	Signature

Date	Keys/Key Fobs Time Out	Keys/Key Fobs Time In	Signature

Date Work Started	Time Work Started	Date Work Completed	Time Work Completed

Work Checked By	Date	Time

Important Notes	

Log/Reference No	Badge No	Authorised By	Date

Contractors Name		Contractors Company Name	

Vehicle Reg No	Phone No / Mobile No	Email Address

Nature Of Work Undertaken		Location / Area Of Work	

Date	Contractor Time In	Contractor Time Out	Signature

Date	Keys/Key Fobs Time Out	Keys/Key Fobs Time In	Signature

Date Work Started	Time Work Started	Date Work Completed	Time Work Completed

Work Checked By		Date	Time

Important Notes	

Log/Reference No	Badge No	Authorised By	Date

Contractors Name		Contractors Company Name	

Vehicle Reg No	Phone No / Mobile No	Email Address

Nature Of Work Undertaken		Location / Area Of Work	

Date	Contractor Time In	Contractor Time Out	Signature

Date	Keys/Key Fobs Time Out	Keys/Key Fobs Time In	Signature

Date Work Started	Time Work Started	Date Work Completed	Time Work Completed

Work Checked By		Date	Time

Important Notes	

Log/Reference No	Badge No	Authorised By	Date

Contractors Name	Contractors Company Name

Vehicle Reg No	Phone No / Mobile No	Email Address

Nature Of Work Undertaken	Location / Area Of Work

Date	Contractor Time In	Contractor Time Out	Signature

Date	Keys/Key Fobs Time Out	Keys/Key Fobs Time In	Signature

Date Work Started	Time Work Started	Date Work Completed	Time Work Completed

Work Checked By	Date	Time

Important Notes	

Log/Reference No	Badge No	Authorised By	Date

Contractors Name	Contractors Company Name

Vehicle Reg No	Phone No / Mobile No	Email Address

Nature Of Work Undertaken	Location / Area Of Work

Date	Contractor Time In	Contractor Time Out	Signature

Date	Keys/Key Fobs Time Out	Keys/Key Fobs Time In	Signature

Date Work Started	Time Work Started	Date Work Completed	Time Work Completed

Work Checked By	Date	Time

Important Notes	

Log/Reference No	Badge No	Authorised By	Date

Contractors Name	Contractors Company Name

Vehicle Reg No	Phone No / Mobile No	Email Address

Nature Of Work Undertaken	Location / Area Of Work

Date	Contractor Time In	Contractor Time Out	Signature

Date	Keys/Key Fobs Time Out	Keys/Key Fobs Time In	Signature

Date Work Started	Time Work Started	Date Work Completed	Time Work Completed

Work Checked By	Date	Time

Important Notes	

Log/Reference No	Badge No	Authorised By	Date

Contractors Name	Contractors Company Name

Vehicle Reg No	Phone No / Mobile No	Email Address

Nature Of Work Undertaken	Location / Area Of Work

Date	Contractor Time In	Contractor Time Out	Signature

Date	Keys/Key Fobs Time Out	Keys/Key Fobs Time In	Signature

Date Work Started	Time Work Started	Date Work Completed	Time Work Completed

Work Checked By	Date	Time

Important Notes	

Log/Reference No	Badge No	Authorised By	Date

Contractors Name	Contractors Company Name

Vehicle Reg No	Phone No / Mobile No	Email Address

Nature Of Work Undertaken	Location / Area Of Work

Date	Contractor Time In	Contractor Time Out	Signature

Date	Keys/Key Fobs Time Out	Keys/Key Fobs Time In	Signature

Date Work Started	Time Work Started	Date Work Completed	Time Work Completed

Work Checked By	Date	Time

Important Notes	

Log/Reference No	Badge No	Authorised By	Date

Contractors Name	Contractors Company Name

Vehicle Reg No	Phone No / Mobile No	Email Address

Nature Of Work Undertaken	Location / Area Of Work

Date	Contractor Time In	Contractor Time Out	Signature

Date	Keys/Key Fobs Time Out	Keys/Key Fobs Time In	Signature

Date Work Started	Time Work Started	Date Work Completed	Time Work Completed

Work Checked By	Date	Time

Important Notes	

Log/Reference No	Badge No	Authorised By	Date

Contractors Name	Contractors Company Name

Vehicle Reg No	Phone No / Mobile No	Email Address

Nature Of Work Undertaken	Location / Area Of Work

Date	Contractor Time In	Contractor Time Out	Signature

Date	Keys/Key Fobs Time Out	Keys/Key Fobs Time In	Signature

Date Work Started	Time Work Started	Date Work Completed	Time Work Completed

Work Checked By	Date	Time

Important Notes	

Log/Reference No	Badge No	Authorised By	Date

Contractors Name	Contractors Company Name

Vehicle Reg No	Phone No / Mobile No	Email Address

Nature Of Work Undertaken	Location / Area Of Work

Date	Contractor Time In	Contractor Time Out	Signature

Date	Keys/Key Fobs Time Out	Keys/Key Fobs Time In	Signature

Date Work Started	Time Work Started	Date Work Completed	Time Work Completed

Work Checked By	Date	Time

Important Notes	

Log/Reference No	Badge No	Authorised By	Date

Contractors Name		Contractors Company Name	

Vehicle Reg No	Phone No / Mobile No	Email Address

Nature Of Work Undertaken		Location / Area Of Work	

Date	Contractor Time In	Contractor Time Out	Signature

Date	Keys/Key Fobs Time Out	Keys/Key Fobs Time In	Signature

Date Work Started	Time Work Started	Date Work Completed	Time Work Completed

Work Checked By		Date	Time

Important Notes	

Log/Reference No	Badge No	Authorised By	Date

Contractors Name		Contractors Company Name	

Vehicle Reg No	Phone No / Mobile No	Email Address

Nature Of Work Undertaken		Location / Area Of Work	

Date	Contractor Time In	Contractor Time Out	Signature

Date	Keys/Key Fobs Time Out	Keys/Key Fobs Time In	Signature

Date Work Started	Time Work Started	Date Work Completed	Time Work Completed

Work Checked By		Date	Time

Important Notes	

Log/Reference No	Badge No	Authorised By	Date

Contractors Name		Contractors Company Name	

Vehicle Reg No	Phone No / Mobile No	Email Address	

Nature Of Work Undertaken		Location / Area Of Work	

Date	Contractor Time In	Contractor Time Out	Signature

Date	Keys/Key Fobs Time Out	Keys/Key Fobs Time In	Signature

Date Work Started	Time Work Started	Date Work Completed	Time Work Completed

Work Checked By		Date	Time

Important Notes	

Log/Reference No	Badge No	Authorised By	Date

Contractors Name		Contractors Company Name	

Vehicle Reg No	Phone No / Mobile No	Email Address	

Nature Of Work Undertaken		Location / Area Of Work	

Date	Contractor Time In	Contractor Time Out	Signature

Date	Keys/Key Fobs Time Out	Keys/Key Fobs Time In	Signature

Date Work Started	Time Work Started	Date Work Completed	Time Work Completed

Work Checked By		Date	Time

Important Notes	

Log/Reference No	Badge No	Authorised By	Date

Contractors Name	Contractors Company Name

Vehicle Reg No	Phone No / Mobile No	Email Address

Nature Of Work Undertaken	Location / Area Of Work

Date	Contractor Time In	Contractor Time Out	Signature

Date	Keys/Key Fobs Time Out	Keys/Key Fobs Time In	Signature

Date Work Started	Time Work Started	Date Work Completed	Time Work Completed

Work Checked By	Date	Time

Important Notes	

Log/Reference No	Badge No	Authorised By	Date

Contractors Name	Contractors Company Name

Vehicle Reg No	Phone No / Mobile No	Email Address

Nature Of Work Undertaken	Location / Area Of Work

Date	Contractor Time In	Contractor Time Out	Signature

Date	Keys/Key Fobs Time Out	Keys/Key Fobs Time In	Signature

Date Work Started	Time Work Started	Date Work Completed	Time Work Completed

Work Checked By	Date	Time

Important Notes	

Log/Reference No	Badge No	Authorised By	Date

Contractors Name	Contractors Company Name

Vehicle Reg No	Phone No / Mobile No	Email Address

Nature Of Work Undertaken	Location / Area Of Work

Date	Contractor Time In	Contractor Time Out	Signature

Date	Keys/Key Fobs Time Out	Keys/Key Fobs Time In	Signature

Date Work Started	Time Work Started	Date Work Completed	Time Work Completed

Work Checked By	Date	Time

Important Notes	

Log/Reference No	Badge No	Authorised By	Date

Contractors Name	Contractors Company Name

Vehicle Reg No	Phone No / Mobile No	Email Address

Nature Of Work Undertaken	Location / Area Of Work

Date	Contractor Time In	Contractor Time Out	Signature

Date	Keys/Key Fobs Time Out	Keys/Key Fobs Time In	Signature

Date Work Started	Time Work Started	Date Work Completed	Time Work Completed

Work Checked By	Date	Time

Important Notes	

Log/Reference No		Badge No		Authorised By		Date	

Contractors Name		Contractors Company Name	

Vehicle Reg No		Phone No / Mobile No		Email Address	

Nature Of Work Undertaken		Location / Area Of Work	

Date	Contractor Time In	Contractor Time Out	Signature

Date	Keys/Key Fobs Time Out	Keys/Key Fobs Time In	Signature

Date Work Started	Time Work Started	Date Work Completed	Time Work Completed

Work Checked By		Date	Time

Important Notes	

Log/Reference No		Badge No		Authorised By		Date	

Contractors Name		Contractors Company Name	

Vehicle Reg No		Phone No / Mobile No		Email Address	

Nature Of Work Undertaken		Location / Area Of Work	

Date	Contractor Time In	Contractor Time Out	Signature

Date	Keys/Key Fobs Time Out	Keys/Key Fobs Time In	Signature

Date Work Started	Time Work Started	Date Work Completed	Time Work Completed

Work Checked By		Date	Time

Important Notes	

Log/Reference No	Badge No	Authorised By	Date

Contractors Name		Contractors Company Name	

Vehicle Reg No	Phone No / Mobile No	Email Address

Nature Of Work Undertaken		Location / Area Of Work	

Date	Contractor Time In	Contractor Time Out	Signature

Date	Keys/Key Fobs Time Out	Keys/Key Fobs Time In	Signature

Date Work Started	Time Work Started	Date Work Completed	Time Work Completed

Work Checked By		Date	Time

Important Notes	

Log/Reference No	Badge No	Authorised By	Date

Contractors Name		Contractors Company Name	

Vehicle Reg No	Phone No / Mobile No	Email Address

Nature Of Work Undertaken		Location / Area Of Work	

Date	Contractor Time In	Contractor Time Out	Signature

Date	Keys/Key Fobs Time Out	Keys/Key Fobs Time In	Signature

Date Work Started	Time Work Started	Date Work Completed	Time Work Completed

Work Checked By		Date	Time

Important Notes	

Log/Reference No	Badge No	Authorised By	Date

Contractors Name	Contractors Company Name

Vehicle Reg No	Phone No / Mobile No	Email Address

Nature Of Work Undertaken	Location / Area Of Work

Date	Contractor Time In	Contractor Time Out	Signature

Date	Keys/Key Fobs Time Out	Keys/Key Fobs Time In	Signature

Date Work Started	Time Work Started	Date Work Completed	Time Work Completed

Work Checked By	Date	Time

Important Notes	

Log/Reference No	Badge No	Authorised By	Date

Contractors Name	Contractors Company Name

Vehicle Reg No	Phone No / Mobile No	Email Address

Nature Of Work Undertaken	Location / Area Of Work

Date	Contractor Time In	Contractor Time Out	Signature

Date	Keys/Key Fobs Time Out	Keys/Key Fobs Time In	Signature

Date Work Started	Time Work Started	Date Work Completed	Time Work Completed

Work Checked By	Date	Time

Important Notes	

Log/Reference No	Badge No	Authorised By	Date

Contractors Name	Contractors Company Name

Vehicle Reg No	Phone No / Mobile No	Email Address

Nature Of Work Undertaken	Location / Area Of Work

Date	Contractor Time In	Contractor Time Out	Signature

Date	Keys/Key Fobs Time Out	Keys/Key Fobs Time In	Signature

Date Work Started	Time Work Started	Date Work Completed	Time Work Completed

Work Checked By	Date	Time

Important Notes	

Log/Reference No	Badge No	Authorised By	Date

Contractors Name	Contractors Company Name

Vehicle Reg No	Phone No / Mobile No	Email Address

Nature Of Work Undertaken	Location / Area Of Work

Date	Contractor Time In	Contractor Time Out	Signature

Date	Keys/Key Fobs Time Out	Keys/Key Fobs Time In	Signature

Date Work Started	Time Work Started	Date Work Completed	Time Work Completed

Work Checked By	Date	Time

Important Notes	

Log/Reference No	Badge No	Authorised By	Date

Contractors Name	Contractors Company Name

Vehicle Reg No	Phone No / Mobile No	Email Address

Nature Of Work Undertaken	Location / Area Of Work

Date	Contractor Time In	Contractor Time Out	Signature

Date	Keys/Key Fobs Time Out	Keys/Key Fobs Time In	Signature

Date Work Started	Time Work Started	Date Work Completed	Time Work Completed

Work Checked By	Date	Time

Important Notes	

Log/Reference No	Badge No	Authorised By	Date

Contractors Name	Contractors Company Name

Vehicle Reg No	Phone No / Mobile No	Email Address

Nature Of Work Undertaken	Location / Area Of Work

Date	Contractor Time In	Contractor Time Out	Signature

Date	Keys/Key Fobs Time Out	Keys/Key Fobs Time In	Signature

Date Work Started	Time Work Started	Date Work Completed	Time Work Completed

Work Checked By	Date	Time

Important Notes	

Log/Reference No	Badge No	Authorised By	Date

Contractors Name		Contractors Company Name	

Vehicle Reg No	Phone No / Mobile No	Email Address

Nature Of Work Undertaken		Location / Area Of Work	

Date	Contractor Time In	Contractor Time Out	Signature

Date	Keys/Key Fobs Time Out	Keys/Key Fobs Time In	Signature

Date Work Started	Time Work Started	Date Work Completed	Time Work Completed

Work Checked By		Date	Time

Important Notes	

Log/Reference No	Badge No	Authorised By	Date

Contractors Name		Contractors Company Name	

Vehicle Reg No	Phone No / Mobile No	Email Address

Nature Of Work Undertaken		Location / Area Of Work	

Date	Contractor Time In	Contractor Time Out	Signature

Date	Keys/Key Fobs Time Out	Keys/Key Fobs Time In	Signature

Date Work Started	Time Work Started	Date Work Completed	Time Work Completed

Work Checked By		Date	Time

Important Notes	

Log/Reference No	Badge No	Authorised By	Date

Contractors Name	Contractors Company Name

Vehicle Reg No	Phone No / Mobile No	Email Address

Nature Of Work Undertaken	Location / Area Of Work

Date	Contractor Time In	Contractor Time Out	Signature

Date	Keys/Key Fobs Time Out	Keys/Key Fobs Time In	Signature

Date Work Started	Time Work Started	Date Work Completed	Time Work Completed

Work Checked By	Date	Time

Important Notes	

Log/Reference No	Badge No	Authorised By	Date

Contractors Name	Contractors Company Name

Vehicle Reg No	Phone No / Mobile No	Email Address

Nature Of Work Undertaken	Location / Area Of Work

Date	Contractor Time In	Contractor Time Out	Signature

Date	Keys/Key Fobs Time Out	Keys/Key Fobs Time In	Signature

Date Work Started	Time Work Started	Date Work Completed	Time Work Completed

Work Checked By	Date	Time

Important Notes	

Log/Reference No	Badge No	Authorised By	Date

Contractors Name	Contractors Company Name

Vehicle Reg No	Phone No / Mobile No	Email Address

Nature Of Work Undertaken	Location / Area Of Work

Date	Contractor Time In	Contractor Time Out	Signature

Date	Keys/Key Fobs Time Out	Keys/Key Fobs Time In	Signature

Date Work Started	Time Work Started	Date Work Completed	Time Work Completed

Work Checked By	Date	Time

Important Notes	

Log/Reference No	Badge No	Authorised By	Date

Contractors Name	Contractors Company Name

Vehicle Reg No	Phone No / Mobile No	Email Address

Nature Of Work Undertaken	Location / Area Of Work

Date	Contractor Time In	Contractor Time Out	Signature

Date	Keys/Key Fobs Time Out	Keys/Key Fobs Time In	Signature

Date Work Started	Time Work Started	Date Work Completed	Time Work Completed

Work Checked By	Date	Time

Important Notes	

Log/Reference No	Badge No	Authorised By	Date

Contractors Name		Contractors Company Name	

Vehicle Reg No		Phone No / Mobile No	Email Address

Nature Of Work Undertaken		Location / Area Of Work	

Date	Contractor Time In	Contractor Time Out	Signature

Date	Keys/Key Fobs Time Out	Keys/Key Fobs Time In	Signature

Date Work Started	Time Work Started	Date Work Completed	Time Work Completed

Work Checked By		Date	Time

Important Notes	

Log/Reference No	Badge No	Authorised By	Date

Contractors Name		Contractors Company Name	

Vehicle Reg No		Phone No / Mobile No	Email Address

Nature Of Work Undertaken		Location / Area Of Work	

Date	Contractor Time In	Contractor Time Out	Signature

Date	Keys/Key Fobs Time Out	Keys/Key Fobs Time In	Signature

Date Work Started	Time Work Started	Date Work Completed	Time Work Completed

Work Checked By		Date	Time

Important Notes	

Log/Reference No	Badge No	Authorised By	Date

Contractors Name	Contractors Company Name

Vehicle Reg No	Phone No / Mobile No	Email Address

Nature Of Work Undertaken	Location / Area Of Work

Date	Contractor Time In	Contractor Time Out	Signature

Date	Keys/Key Fobs Time Out	Keys/Key Fobs Time In	Signature

Date Work Started	Time Work Started	Date Work Completed	Time Work Completed

Work Checked By	Date	Time

Important Notes	

Log/Reference No	Badge No	Authorised By	Date

Contractors Name	Contractors Company Name

Vehicle Reg No	Phone No / Mobile No	Email Address

Nature Of Work Undertaken	Location / Area Of Work

Date	Contractor Time In	Contractor Time Out	Signature

Date	Keys/Key Fobs Time Out	Keys/Key Fobs Time In	Signature

Date Work Started	Time Work Started	Date Work Completed	Time Work Completed

Work Checked By	Date	Time

Important Notes	

"Thank you for being an exceptional customer."

We hope that your notebook exceeded your expectations.

Creating notebook ideas is what we do.

Notebooks designed with love for you and your business.

If you have any notebook ideas, big or small, we would love to hear from you.

And maybe we can make those ideas come to life!

Additional pages adding?
New features or sections creating?
Other notebook sizes?
Any covers or page design ideas?
Any industries or sectors you require notebooks for?

Please email any notebook suggestions to:

sales@FyldeMerchandise.com

www.FyldeMerchandise.com